Parenting

in your own

Voice

Parenting
in your own
Voice

Finding Your Inner Parent
to Bring Out the Best in Your Child

Joan L. Reynolds, MS
Sheila Dinaburg-Azoff, PsyD

Cover and text design by Elizabeth Cline.

Significant discounts for bulk sales are available. Please contact Joan and Sheila at info@parentinginyourownvoice@com.

Free downloadable templates of selected exercises, assessments, and worksheets are available at the companion website: www.parentinginyourownvoice.com.

CONTENTS

Appendices

INTRODUCTION

Nothing quite prepared us for the realities of becoming someone's parent. Advanced degrees and years of professional experience working with children didn't mean that we, as parents, worried less, trusted our instincts more, or felt confident when the unexpected happened. Joan remembers feeling so anxious in the early years that she resolutely parented "by the book," even when the book didn't seem to work. Sheila frequently found herself yearning for a "Ten-Step Path" or the perfect list of "Guiding Parenting Principles" that would ground and direct her when she felt overwhelmed or lost.

Like so many other parents scouring the parenting section of their local bookstores and libraries, we were looking for direction and confidence from experts who knew more than we did. It never occurred to us, then, that the most important resource we needed, we already had (reflected back at us every day in the mirror). Inside us was a wise inner parent waiting to be recognized.

Gratefully, our stories didn't end there. Our individual journeys, as professionals and parents, continued as we raised our daughters and worked with many more children and their parents. Over and over we saw the simple truths that parents wanted to do their best, but too often felt lost, and children wanted to be seen, but too often felt unseen. In somewhat different arenas—Joan as a learning specialist and Sheila as a pediatric psychologist—our work involved helping children and parents find the success they both wanted and needed.

In addition to the similar commitments the two of us shared, our ideas and principles followed parallel paths. We were like-minded in our respect for the inner wisdom of parents, the power of the parent-child bond, and the value of a child's individuality. As parents, we were each working on connecting to our deep inner knowing, or voice, that guided us toward what was right and best for our children and ourselves. The more we understood ourselves and our children and what was important to us, the clearer we became in our actions and decision making. Then, as we helped parents bolster their inner knowing with helpful information about how a child grows and thrives, and why each is happily different from one another, we found that they too gained confidence and ease in their parenting.

When our individual work brought us together and then evolved into a book collaboration, we agreed that we didn't want to be experts giving parenting advice, but rather guides, helping others find and trust *their* inner parent. Your inner parent is your connection to your internal knowing voice, that part of you that knows what is important to you, and sees your child with a clear eye and a compassionate heart. *Parenting in Your Own Voice* is the book we would have liked when we were struggling with our parenting—not a manual that outlines parenting goals or priorities but a workbook that helps you create your destination and chart your own course.

Blending Sheila's pediatric psychology experience and Joan's learning specialist background, we developed a process designed to help you confidently make consistent decisions and set clear intentions for parenting. Your decisions and intentions won't be based on what we think or what an expert advises, but on your own values and priorities, and on the needs, qualities, and issues unique to your child. By the end of this hands-on process, you will have your own personal touchstones to guide you and a practical plan for what you can do every day.

The workbook format is organized into three thematic parts that build on one another and reinforce your framework of knowledge, understanding, and purpose. The twelve chapters, with exercises peppered throughout, are rich in information and insights, but short on time demands. This way, you can read or work through a single chapter in one sitting or one parent group meeting. With the help of engaging activities, you will delve into yourself and your child, try on new ways of thinking, and acquire a whole new toolkit of resources and strategies. Abundant examples of real parents and children bring it all to life, though the names used are fictitious.

Our personal and work experiences convince us that effective parenting begins not with a focus on the child, but on oneself. That's why Part I of this workbook is all about you—finding your unique voice, learning about the nine temperament traits that make your nature different from everyone else's, identifying your values and what's important to you, and finally, remembering what makes you feel happy and fulfilled.

Part II shifts the focus onto your child. You see her in the context of development, observe her talents and interests, and come to understand how and why she learns some things more easily than others. You also explore your *child's* nature using those same nine temperament traits from Part I, and then see how they compare with yours, side by side. This is a section of surprises and aha moments as your newly honed observation and listening skills help you take in who your child is—without judgments, expectations, or other distortions. With the completion of Part II you will have a detailed, multifaceted picture of your child, along with insights and ideas that will help you parent to her unique needs and gifts.

Part III is where you identify your direction—where you want to go in terms of what you most want for your child and what you feel is most important for him now and in the future. Here is where you integrate what you've learned about yourself with what you've learned about your child to create your own parenting plan. This plan, which serves as a template, can be altered and updated as your child grows and changes. It will help you make decisions that are aligned with *your* parenting priorities and understanding of your child and informed by *your* individual voice.

The book winds down with a chapter that reminds us of ways to enjoy and embrace the experience of being a parent, with stories of parents finding their inner parent and parenting in their own voice.

If you are feeling worried, unsure of yourself, or overwhelmed, we hope by the end of *Parenting in Your Own Voice* that you too will feel more directed and self-assured. Armed with fresh ways to think about yourself and your child, you will have a new awareness that helps you parent with consciousness, intention, and acceptance.

We facilitate *Parenting in Your Own Voice* workshops in upstate New York, where we live and work. Our process can be used by parents and caregivers with children of every age. In writing this workbook, it is our hope that parents will come together in their own communities and create small parenting groups. *(See "How to Use This Book.")* Joan and Sheila are available to help you jumpstart your own *Parenting in Your Own Voice* workshops. You can contact us by email at info@parentinginyourownvoice.com.

We believe a future filled with hope and promise is possible when children manifest their individual potential. This is the work of parenting and the aim of *Parenting in Your Own Voice.*

—Sheila Dinaburg-Azoff and Joan Reynolds, Woodstock, New York

HOW TO USE THIS BOOK

When we first developed the format for *Parenting in Your Own Voice,* we envisioned small groups of parents meeting regularly to share insights and questions that arose from reading the book and completing the exercises. We know that working in groups provides parents a much appreciated support system and the encouragement to see activities through to completion.

Of course, being part of a parenting group is not right or possible for everyone. You may choose to read the book and work through the process on your own or with a coparent, grandparent, or other caregiver. However you decide to use the book, go at your own pace and make it work for you. That might mean you read it all the way through once and then go back and do the exercises on a second read-through, or that you decide to read the book without doing any of the exercises. Everyone will get something out of the book, but the more involved you become, the more you'll benefit.

Each chapter has exercises and activities that enable you to dig deeper into the topic, broaden your perspective, and generate great discussions. (Have a pen handy!) Some of the chapters ask that you fill out an assessment on you or your child, and some have short writing assignments, the answers to which become components of the parenting plan you'll assemble in Chapter 11. If you skip these, you won't have the building blocks you'll need later.

For groups, we recommend doing one chapter per meeting (unless you'd like to linger and delve deeper into a subject). We placed this symbol next to an exercise or "Try This" activity in each chapter as a trigger for group discussion. If you're having trouble getting group members to share, especially in the beginning, these discussion prompts can be helpful.

However, it's been our experience that when a group of parents gets together to talk about their kids, there's usually no shortage of discussion topics.

This workbook is for parents with children of all ages and stages who want to learn more about themselves and their children, and wish to create a personal approach for parenting. Going through the process provides a framework for thinking about how and why you make your parenting decisions. The many areas of exploration are naturally limited, so take advantage of the good resources provided in Appendix 4 whenever a particular topic sparks your interest.

It is also quite possible that you will come upon a topic or area that makes you think you might benefit from the help of a professional. We encourage you to trust that instinct.

Downloadable Templates

We have provided free downloadable templates of essential assessments and exercises at our website, www.parentinginyourownvoice.com, where you can print out as many copies as you need. All of the exercises and assessments in the chapters that follow are designed for one parent and one child. If you're doing this workbook with a coparent or other caregiver, or if you have more than one child, you'll need extra copies of the worksheets. If you're leading or hosting a parenting group, you might want to print out worksheets ahead of time for group members. Also, we know some of you can't bear writing in books, so we've saved you the discomfort!

We're Here to Help

We're available to help your group once you've assembled its members. We're delighted to provide some initial coaching so your group can launch out on its own and be self-guiding and self-sufficient, or to facilitate and guide it along the way. If you would like advice or help getting a small parenting group going using the *Parenting in Your Own Voice* process, please contact us at info@parentinginyourownvoice.com.

Part 1

Who Am I?

Part I of this workbook is devoted to you—getting reacquainted with your inner wisdom and intuition, your unique temperament, the values you live by, and the interests and activities that feed you and make **you** happy.

As a parent, you have acquired another identity—that of "Annabelle's mom" or "Jason's dad." The first time someone introduces you like that, it may sound foreign to you. But pretty soon you may come to see your world through the lens of being your child's parent. That's natural, because raising a child is an all-consuming endeavor, and your life after kids is never quite the same.

Nevertheless, in our professions and in our parenting workshops, we have found that the best way to become a more effective parent is to focus first on *yourself,* apart from your children. Once you get firmly grounded in your own shoes, you can turn your attention to your child and your parenting vision. The exercises, activities, and discussion guides in Part I are designed to help you revisit who you are and what's important for your life.

In the first chapter, you will learn about the concept of *voice,* your internal guidance system that will lead you to the truth and the right decision. You will practice getting good at hearing and heeding it. Chapter 2 will take you through a fun and enlightening self-discovery process that helps you map out your unique temperament along nine traits. You will come to see how those traits shape who you are and impact your behavior. In Chapter 3, you will examine your personal values and think about how they affect your decisions and attitudes now, and how you would like them to guide your future. The last chapter puts you back in touch with the person you are besides being Annabelle's mom or Jason's dad. It encourages you to grow, develop, explore, play, and have more fun. The parenting benefit is that you have more energy and ways to give.

Your Voice

What is *voice?* Voice is the most important tool you have for being true to yourself as an individual and as a parent. Voice is your inner wisdom: your insights, knowing, perceptions, instincts, intuition, and feelings. It is how you come to know yourself. Like an internal guidance system, with the destination permanently programmed to "what's right for me," your voice communicates through physical sensations, inner murmurings, flashes of insights, and compelling hunches. That gut feeling something is right, the "aha" moment, the inexplicable urge to do something out of character, or the hair standing up on the back of your neck—these are all voice guiding you to your best action.

If your idea of voice feels a bit fuzzy, don't worry. Soon enough, you'll have your own experience of what voice means and how it guides you. We'll help you by offering ways to recognize your unique voice and practice listening for it. You'll get a sense of voice through the experiences of others; you'll explore body cues and identify obstacles—the ones that prevent you from hearing "the small still voice" and the ones that discourage you from trusting or following it.

The process of using your voice for guidance is one you will hone in this chapter, and then practice using throughout the workbook and in your life. The better you get at tuning in to it, the more reliable and trustworthy it becomes.

Recognizing Your Voice

Most parents we meet at the beginning of our workshops have a sense of what voice is and are able to share anecdotes about times when they listened to it—and made good decisions. Just as often parents tell us stories about when not listening to their voice resulted in a bad decision. At times, we all ignore our voice, tune it out, or simply get distracted. An important step in listening to our voice is distinguishing it from the obstacles and distractions that get in the way.

Voice vs. Chatter

Part of your internal landscape is the ongoing monologue running through your head at any given moment. We call it "chatter," but chatter is not your voice. It is the constant stream of musings, anxieties, reactions, future fantasies, or feelings of doubt that distract you from your voice. Chatter can be critical or glowing, making you look backwards ("Why did I do that?" or "She thinks I'm wonderful"). Sometimes it's rooted in the future, carrying feelings of worry or excitement ("I hope my speech will be well received" or "I'll see her at the airport"). And sometimes chatter is merely random noise.

Whatever the content of our chatter is, it keeps us out of the present moment and distances us from our voice. When we practice stillness and become conscious of the foreground noise of our chatter, it naturally quiets. Then, with the static turned down, our voice can be "heard."

Here are two exercises that will help you become more aware of your chatter—the first step to hearing your voice.

EXERCISE: CATCHING THE CHATTER.

The purpose of this exercise is to stop and take notice of your inner chatter. Get a pen and pad, and sit in a comfy chair in a quiet room. Have a clock with a second hand and get ready to sit still for three to four minutes. Close your eyes. Imagine that you have a butterfly net that can scoop up any thoughts or feelings or images that come into your conscious mind. As you "catch the chatter," open your eyes and write down a key word about it on your pad. Then shut your eyes again and keep going until you're ready to stop. Were you surprised at how active your mind was? Was there a pattern to your chatter (i.e., to-do lists, regrets, judgments, or song lyrics playing repeatedly) or was it just disconnected thoughts?

EXERCISE: EMBRACING THE BIG NOTHING.

The purpose of this exercise is to show you one way to practice quieting the chatter. Find a comfortable position in a chair or lying down so you don't have to move your body for three to five minutes. Close your eyes, start to breathe deeply, and imagine a chalkboard with the word NOTHING written across it. Focus on that word. Try to keep nothing but NOTHING from entering your mind. Every time a thought, feeling, or image distracts you from the word, refocus on the big NOTHING. Did you get a sense of how it felt to quiet the chatter?

What Voice *IS*

Voice is your guide in the lifelong process of learning about yourself. "Knowing who you are" implies that you cannot be just anybody. It implies individuality. Just as a snowflake has no other like it, you were born to be one-of-a-kind. The quality of your life depends on coming to know your one-of-a-kindness and following its design.

Don't expect bells and whistles, or loud announcements. Many call it "the small still voice within," for its subtle nature. Remember how it was when your child was an infant? At first, all of her crying sounded alike. Later, with lots of crying experiences under your belt, you noticed that different needs resulted in different crying patterns. The "I'm hungry" cry sounded different from the "I need a nap" cry. Voice is like that. At first, you may not even be aware of the gentle sensations and small reactions, or the urge to do one thing or another. Over time, and with careful attention, you will hear your internal language in a more nuanced and related way. Experience will teach you that there is a reliable connection between what's going on inside you and your best choice or action. You will come to know that a sense of fullness around your heart or an overall sense of lightness indicates a good choice for yourself. On the other hand, an uncomfortable stomach, a vague sense of unease, or tight muscles say that something about this situation is not right.

Some of you may wonder: What voice? With no direct experience to draw on, you feel at a loss when you think about tuning into something you never knew existed. It is quite possible that you grew up in a situation where your voice was disregarded or denied. Instead of learning to view your instincts and feelings as valid, you learned to look outside yourself for answers. Take heart. Your internal guidance system is still operating. As you begin to focus on voice, you'll find that it will make itself known. Your awareness of voice gets stronger the more you practice tuning in to it.

Voice as Individual Guide

Your voice is your wisdom and authority, and it often expresses itself through body cues. Body awareness provides important feedback to our real feelings and right choices. A sweaty palm, aches and pains, numbness, a sense of lightness, or a surge of energy all give us information.

Consider some of these stories of voice and how it provided just the right guidance.

> As much as Angie was tempted by the salary and prestige of the job offer, her gut told a different story. When she thought about the type of company it was and the personality of the woman who would be her new boss, her stomach got tied up in knots. Her body already knew what her mind had not yet accepted. This wasn't a good fit.

> When Paul needed to decide between two perfectly good apartments, he found a quiet spot and "checked in." After some slow breathing he imagined himself in each of the apartments, walking into each room, peering out the windows, strolling through the neighborhood. After a few minutes he knew. When he visualized one of the apartments, his heart rate slowed a bit, his muscles relaxed, and he had an overall feeling of peacefulness and letting go. In other words, he felt at home.

We know sometimes without understanding how we know. It's the phenomenon that Malcolm Gladwell describes in his book, *Blink,* and scientists have tried to understand by studying behavior and the brain. Our uncanny ability to respond without consciously thinking is not magic or just luck. It's the way we're wired and it's ours to use if we tune in and trust it.

> A soldier in Iraq sensed an IED without full awareness of what tipped him off. To this day he can't say how he "just knew" the hidden bomb was there.

Lenny was driving 65 mph down the interstate when the thought popped into his head that he should change lanes, which he did. A few minutes later, the car that had been behind him rear-ended the car in front of it. Had he not changed lanes it could have been Lenny's car that got hit.

Intuition, instincts, hunches, compelling reactions, feeling drawn to something immediately and intensely—all of these sensations are worthy of our attention. If we consciously connect with them, then we can also consciously consider whether they feel right.

Barbara encountered a woman she had met months before, and with whom she felt little connection. They chatted for a few minutes about new work, homes, and kids, and then went their separate ways. Inexplicably, Barbara felt a compelling sense of urgency to contact this woman again. She did, and for the next five years they ended up collaborating on a project together.

Patty was thrilled with the offer of a promotion and a pay raise. The job was right up her alley, with travel opportunities and an exciting challenge in a cutting-edge technology. It got her heart racing just thinking about it.

TRY THIS: *See if you can "feel the pull" of your voice over the next few days. For example, notice in a group situation which people you were drawn to talk to, and how that felt. Pay attention to small impulses you might have, like the urge to call a particular friend. Don't think about why you made these choices. Just become more aware of how it feels to be subtly pulled in one direction over another. This is your voice guiding you.*

Remember Patty from above, excited about a new job prospect? There was one big problem: Her daughter, Beth, had numerous special needs

that demanded a lot of nighttime assistance, and the job required her
to be away from home two nights a week. Beth's dad mostly took her
on the weekends and knew little about the weekday routines. A few
sleepless nights later, Patty realized she would regret it forever if she
didn't try to find a way to make the new job work. Once she decided
to go for it, things just flowed. Her ex liked the idea of more time with
Beth; her boss agreed to a three-month trial period; and when they
found a new daycare with extended hours, it happened to have a staff
member trained in working with special needs children.

A sure sign that your actions are aligned with voice is the sense of flow that follows—like Patty deciding to take a job that seemed right for her. When she made up her mind to go forward, everything just seemed to fall into place and align with her decision—as if she were cruising down a boulevard with no red lights. Eastern writers refer to the experience as stepping into the Tao—the river of energy that is the center of your life and carries you forward along your path. If you have ever had an experience where you picked up a book, went to a workshop, or met someone new, and that experience then led you to other personally relevant experiences, people, or ideas, then you too have experienced being in the flow.

Voice as Parenting Guide

When you know yourself and act in sync with what you know, you are comfortable in your own skin. You feel directed, satisfied, and confident in your choices. This feeling of comfort and confidence naturally flows and gives integrity to your parenting.

Think of voice as a parenting compass. When you want help with a sticky situation, a difficult decision, or an important action, your voice is always available for guidance and reassurance.

These next stories illustrate the importance of voice as a parenting guide.

A young mom, Bobby Jo, had a strong sense that her ten-month-old son, Max, was ill. After a quick checkup, the pediatrician said her baby was fine. Bobby Jo went home but could not shake the nagging feeling that Max was too sluggish, not himself. While thinking, "I'm just an anxious mom," she had a deep, unrelenting feeling that would not let her rest. She just KNEW something was not right with Max. After she insisted on another office exam, the doctor complied, and sure enough, he detected a problem that could have become serious if left untreated.

Prior to Ellie going into third grade, her best friend's parents requested the teacher with a reputation for being academically rigorous. After visiting all the third-grade classrooms, Ellie's mom, Tammy, felt drawn to a different teacher, sensing that her style and the classroom atmosphere would be a better fit for Ellie. Despite pressure from the other mom to keep the girls together, Tammy requested the teacher who seemed to be the better choice for Ellie. It turned out to be a great fit, and Ellie thrived socially and academically.

Tuning In and Connecting to Your Voice

As we said earlier, in order to tune in and hear your voice, you must first quiet the chatter that distracts you. When you did the exercises, "Catching the Chatter" and "Embracing the Big Nothing," you may have experienced that this simple task is actually quite difficult. To get better at tuning in requires that you practice staying in the present moment—no past obsessing and reliving, and no future worrying and planning. Luckily, you have a readily available tool to help—your breath.

EXERCISE: BREATHING INTO THE PRESENT.

This simple breath-focusing exercise is the easiest way to reset your mind to the present and get into a calm, quiet state. Be silent and still. Now, focus on the "in" breath as the cool air fills your nostrils and then continues down to fill your stomach like a balloon being inflated. Deflate the balloon on the "out" breath and follow it as it exhales out your nose as a warm breath. Do it a couple of times and see if your mind feels quieter.

Notice that the instructions for the above exercise did not say, "Find a silent place," but rather, "Be silent." To be present in any circumstance (meditating, eating, walking, listening, etc.) you need to silence the chatter inside, not the sounds of life outside. Sound, or what some may call noise, cannot be avoided. When external silence is not a requirement, your practice can happen anywhere: in the noisy train station, the doctor's waiting room, the car stalled in traffic, or the corner of a room in a busy household. It is not easy, but it *is* possible.

Start with one moment at a time, recognizing that in the beginning, no one is able to do this for more than a few moments. Our mind likes to wander and be distracted. You will naturally slip into chatter, so when you do, no big deal. Just notice it, name it if you like, and then try again to be present in the moment. Do it as long as you can or have time for, but keep practicing. Make friends with the stillness and silence. You'll get better, and your ability to quiet your mind will improve. When you quiet your mind, your life gets less hectic, your thoughts get clearer, and your voice gets stronger.

In addition to staying in the present, *awareness,* or focused attention, is the other key to tuning into your voice. Once the mind is quiet, it is awareness that connects you to your voice. You notice the subtle sensations, gentle stirrings, and quiet thoughts. The wisdom of your voice is available to guide you.

Excessive "busyness" makes awareness difficult. Overloaded schedules, multitasking, and ever-increasing technologies make it much harder to focus on what is before us or inside us. What good is all our productivity if our children feel unseen, our lives feel overwhelming, or we feel lost to ourselves? Slow down, unplug, go inside yourself, and listen. In the same way you quieted the chatter, you nurture awareness with stillness and silence. When you are still and your mind is quiet, your voice will speak to you.

Everyone is different. Experiment and find out what helps you hear your voice. For some people, it's hitting the snooze button in the morning and spending five minutes paying attention to the ideas and impressions coming into one's sleepy brain. For others, it may be meditation or taking a walk or a swim. Setting aside a few minutes before sleep works for others.

Here are three more quick ways to practice tuning in and connecting to your voice.

EXERCISE: GIVING YOURSELF A ONE-MINUTE TUNE-UP.

Stop what you're doing! Put one hand on your heart and one on your stomach. Close your eyes and breathe deeply from your stomach until you feel your body quiet down. Take a quick scan of your body, from the top of your head to your toes. Where do you feel tension? Keep breathing deeply. Why do you feel tension there? Make a mental note of whatever pops into your mind. Sometimes, your voice will reveal an interesting detail that is begging for attention. For example, you notice your neck is stiff. Who or what is being a "pain in the neck" to you right now?

EXERCISE: "SHRINKING" YOURSELF.

Lie down on a couch or bed and look up at the ceiling. If it's helpful to imagine Dr. Freud sitting across the room taking notes, by all means do it! Take two or three deep breaths. Now ask yourself, "What am I feeling?"

Turn inward and become aware of your feelings. What is your answer? Say it out loud. Now ask yourself clarifying questions like, "What do I think those feelings are about?" Pause in silence and listen for the answer. Often your voice will respond by having a thought or word pop into your head. Even if it sounds crazy, give it consideration. Keep asking questions and listening for a few more minutes, remembering to check in and notice shifts in physical sensations and stirrings. Even if you are not rewarded with great insight today, you have practiced tuning inward. Now you are pointed in the right direction to connect to your voice.

EXERCISE: GIVING YOURSELF A FIVE-SENSE BREAK.
The purpose of doing this simple activity is to bring you into the present moment, where voice resides. Go outside and be perfectly still for a moment. Zoom in on each of your five sensory perceptions. What do you see, hear, smell, feel, and taste? Any activity that connects you to your senses is good practice for learning how to be present, right here, right now, so you have the opportunity to experience your voice.

Following Your Voice

As reliable and right as our voice is, why is it we so often ignore it? The simple answer is, we're human. Emotional needs, fears, and borrowed beliefs all have the power to override or combat the wisdom of our voice. These obstacles and pitfalls will always be present, but we can get better at recognizing and diminishing their influence.

The first step to following your voice is seeing the challenges that get in YOUR way. When you identify the ones that trip you up, and then pay attention, you are better able to avoid their pull.

Voice's Competitors and Saboteurs

Here are some of the most common reasons we resist, override, or just plain ignore the wise guidance of our voice:

- **Social, familial, and cultural pressures.** The discomfort of being different is hard for many of us. Expectations for acceptable behavior, beliefs, and attitudes are often dictated and enforced by the larger community of family or society. Acting on your voice may feel threatening or alienating to the larger group. Disapproval, punishment, even isolation may be the price you pay.

  Sandra felt a strong connection with a Muslim classmate but derailed the budding friendship, knowing her family would not accept it.

- **Shoulds and should nots.** Each of us has an internal "rule book" of what we should or should not do or be. Even though these rules originate outside of us, they become a part of our belief system. Thinking about doing something that breaks one of our rules feels so wrong that it overshadows our voice.

  Geri was in competition for a highly prized promotion. Her gut told her to show interest and initiative by highlighting her qualifications to her boss. But self-promotion felt like bragging, and bragging was something you "should not" do in Geri's rule book.

- **Discomfort with conflict.** Everyone has different levels of comfort with conflict, but we can all relate to dreading confrontation or disagreeable encounters. Aggressive behavior, criticism from loved ones, or situations where someone's feelings might get hurt are often hard to tolerate. For some, any conflict is scary and stressful. When anxiety is high, our need to avoid conflict can easily silence our voice.

Kathy was overloaded at work and home. A huge birthday party was not what she or her daughter wanted. Even so, she planned a party for the entire first-grade class, just to avoid calls from angry or upset parents whose children did not get invited.

- **Emotional discomfort.** We have a natural aversion to emotional discomfort. We avoid frustration, disappointment, discontent, and most of all, disapproval in our own lives, and then we shield our children from these enemies of happiness. Our self-esteem may even feel at risk when our children struggle or we encounter disapproval. Voice has a strong tide to swim against when it guides us toward emotional discomfort.

  Jake was grounded for good cause when the invitation arrived to join a friend's family for a weekend ski trip. As Jake begged for this "once in a lifetime" opportunity, his dad, Sidney, felt torn. Jake's promises to do better and his pleading for reconsideration were hard to resist. Sidney said yes, despite his voice yelling NO!

- **Resistance to change.** While some may embrace change in their lives, many more find it stressful—even threatening. When we perceive change as the cause of losing control or losing what is comfortable and familiar, our instinct is to put on the brakes and turn off our voice.

  Corey lived in his apartment for twelve years. Even though the landlord was negligent, the neighborhood didn't suit him, and the heat was erratic, it was still home. When friends encouraged him to consider another part of town where there were more people his age, a park, and great restaurants, he decided to consider it. The perfect apartment came available, but suddenly Corey was no longer sure. The new place felt great, but the truth was, he couldn't imagine leaving his longtime home.

- **Strong desires or fantasies.** Sometimes a deep emotional need distorts our reality. We write the perfect script or fantasy for a relationship, experience, or situation and become blinded to anything that may interfere with our story line. As a result, outside advice, contrary evidence, or the internal rumblings of our voice are quickly dismissed or ignored.

  Alex met Sarah and was sure she was the one for him. He had waited a long time for a relationship, and the romantic in him imagined a long happy future together. Nothing was going to spoil it. Not the pangs of hurt he felt when Sarah was sarcastic, or the knots in his stomach when she argued her point without listening to his. All the little red flares his voice sent up were explained away, denied, or simply ignored to protect the fantasy relationship he longed for.

- **Projecting into the future.** Fears and anxiety take us out of the present moment. When this happens we put on our "fortune teller" turbans and make predictions about the future. Convinced, we then make decisions based on these assumptions. Our urgency to control the outcome overrides any attention we might pay to voice.

  David had a big paper due just before the end of the semester that would count for a third of his English grade. His mother panicked when it looked as though he wasn't going to complete it on time. First she imagined the bad grade and then pictured it going out on all his college applications and ruining his chances for a badly needed scholarship. What choice did she have but to do some of the research herself and make sure the paper got done?

So, when you're really struggling to hear your voice, pay attention to the chatter, identify the assumptions and fears getting in your way, and notice what your body cues are trying to tell you. Then see what feels right.

Voice's Imposters

At some time or another everyone is bound to be confused by a message they think is their voice—what we call "voice's imposters." Often, very strong emotional reactions or feelings can be mistaken for voice. It's helpful to remain open to the possibility that you may be listening to an emotional voice imposter.

Any time you feel confused about the "rightness" of a decision you've made or are about to make, try this "getting to voice" process. It's a five-step process designed to help you screen out biases, assumptions, emotional reactions, defenses, chatter, and other "noise" so you can clarify what your real and authentic voice is saying.

---> GETTING TO VOICE

1. Remain open and curious.

2. Focus on your body and see if you can identify any physical sensations that are present in this moment.

3. Tune in to them. What's the feeling saying to you? (For example, *I'm afraid. I feel guilty. This doesn't feel right.*)

4. Ask yourself what's causing the feeling. (For example, external pressures, worries about what others will think, negative or self-sabotaging emotions, an urgency/insistence/compulsion to act NOW.)

5. Now, try to locate your true and authentic voice, the one that's pointing you in a direction that feels right. Your voice is the quiet, grounded, knowing one.

Balancing Voices

Parents frequently ask us how two parents can listen to their individual voices and then coparent. To a large extent it is no different from negotiating other important decisions in a relationship. The "Getting to Voice" process, above, is a particularly effective tool to use when coparents disagree. It helps us to speak clearly from our voice and fend off potential feelings or reactions that distort our voice's message. For example, it's common for coparents to feel competitive with each other or defensive about their respective positions. Such reactions can muddle the decision-making process and get in the way of following our voice and making sound decisions. We notice that when couples go through a process of relaxing control, sorting through feelings, and connecting to their voice, there is frequently more agreement than they expected. Come to the discussion with an open mind and heart, remembering that parenting is not a competition with winners and losers—both of you have the best interests of your child in mind.

Here's how the process worked for Tammy and her husband Allan. (Tammy was the mom trying to decide about the best classroom environment for third grader Ellie.)

Tammy's gut or voice said the more laid-back teacher was best for Ellie. Her husband, Allan, wanted the teacher with the tougher reputation because he thought it was important Ellie be challenged. When

Tammy and Allan realized they didn't agree, they individually went through their "getting to voice" process. Once Tammy acknowledged that she was locked in a bit of a power struggle with Allan, she was better able to connect with her gut feelings and put them into words. Her preference was based on the fact that Ellie was most cooperative and responded best in a relaxed warm atmosphere. The more academically rigorous teacher had a structured, no-nonsense approach to teaching. Allan realized in his process that when he considered academic rigor, "should" loomed large. He also noticed his concerns about lack of discipline and a bit of competitiveness with Tammy. It was Allan who ended up changing his mind. He realized his position was based more on apprehension and appearances and less on his voice. When he thought about Ellie, he realized that Tammy was right about the environment that best suited her.

While this process is helpful for all coparenting situations, it is, not surprisingly, less successful for parents who are no longer together and may have poor communication. In many shared-custody situations, relations are strained and a two-sided process of reflection and communication may not be possible. Instead, accept that you only have control over your choices and your own relationship with your child.

Consider Carol and Dick, who went through an acrimonious divorce:

Dick takes his parent responsibilities very seriously and Carol often takes the laissez-faire attitude that kids mostly raise themselves, like she did. When their teenage daughter Libby is with Carol, most anything goes. Then, when she is with Dick, she resents his restrictions and structure. It took time, but Dick finally stopped trying to get Carol to create and enforce limits for Libby. Instead, he paid close attention to his own reactions and attitudes toward Libby, reflecting on his experiences in a journal. He tried to sort out his "shoulds" and his own anger, frustration, and resentment from his voice. When he felt clear, he met with Libby. He spoke from his heart about what was important to him and shared his recent awareness that sometimes his restrictions didn't have much basis. Libby responded affectionately to Dick's honesty, vulnerability, and willingness to change. Together they created an agreement that sounded good to both of them.

When you want to be heard, speak from your voice (read: *heart*) and call in all you've learned about good communication. Then apply those helpful listening skills to your discussion. Dick, operating as a single parent, used the "getting to voice" process for himself and communicated directly with his daughter.

One way to get better at listening to your coparent's voice is to try this next activity.

EXERCISE: REVERSING VOICES.

Think about a recent situation when your voice told you to do one thing, and your spouse's told him or her another. Grrr! Not only did it make you mad, but you knew your spouse was "wrong." Just for fun, step inside your spouse's voice and write down or say why his or her perspective is the right one. No snarkiness allowed. Give it a fair and honest effort. (This activity is a great one to do together—especially in moments of conflict.)

To conclude, getting to know your authentic voice and having it there as a constant guide helps you be a calmer, more confident individual and parent. When your own voice is strong, the distinction between your self and your child's self is clear. If you understand and respect who you are, you are less likely to confuse your feelings, dreams, and talents with what your child feels, desires, or is good at.

CHAPTER *1* TAKE-AWAYS

- We have a hard-wired internal guidance system that is aligned with our true self and tuned to our best interests. It is called voice.

- If you learn to recognize voice, you can practice tuning in to it. The more you practice listening to your voice, the stronger it gets.

- There is another inner monologue going on inside your head, called chatter. Chatter is the static that gets in the way of voice by taking you out of the present moment, where voice resides.

- Voice communicates through body cues. A clenched stomach or tightened shoulders are examples of how voice is trying to alert you to something important.

- Trusting your voice takes practice.

- Cultural norms, the expectations of others, strong emotions or reactions, and fear of change often stand in the way of your ability to hear your voice. By learning to identify these obstacles in the moment, you will get better at tuning in to your voice.

- One of the most difficult things for parents to do is to blend their voices. Try to honor and respect your coparent's voice. It may not be as out of sync with your own as you think.

- Voice is the most important tool you have for being true to yourself as an individual and as a parent. If you can learn to listen to your voice, you will be less afraid to try new parenting approaches, and more able to trust yourself and your decisions.

My Notes and Questions

Your Nature

Like our voice, we are born with a certain nature or pattern of temperament traits that helps define who we are. These traits explain much about our behavior—like why we typically do what we do, or are more comfortable in one situation than another. Parents love it when we explain the connection between our behavior and our temperament. It is as if a door of understanding opens. From then on, we begin to appreciate that many of our actions, reactions, and feelings are natural and predictable for us. We are also better able to make choices that are in alignment with our individual needs.

In this chapter you will learn about nine temperament traits and participate in the enlightening experience of discovering your own nature. Once you have a feel for each of the temperament traits, there are exercises that help you think about your own nature and what makes you tick. The result is a temperament profile that offers direction for keeping your life and temperament in sync. Working through the exercises may also help you feel more accepting of who you are. This is a crucial first step to respecting your child's unique nature and to parenting with his temperament in mind.

What Is Temperament?

During the 1950s and '60s, amidst a surge in research, psychologists moved away from the notion that babies arrived like blank slates, to be molded by parents and shaped by environment. Through careful observation, they noticed that every child possessed his own individual programming—his unique way of reacting to the world around him. (If you have more than one child, you've probably already noticed this.)

Dr. Stella Chess was one of the professionals who turned her attention to understanding these innate differences in children. Along with Drs. Thomas and Birch, she analyzed years of observations, working to categorize the similarities and differences in human behavior they witnessed. The results: a list of nine traits shared by all, to one degree or another.

---> THE NINE TEMPERAMENT TRAITS

Here are nine traits, or typical ways of behaving and reacting, as described by Drs. Chess, Thomas, and Birch:

1. **Activity Level:** the amount of physical movement you typically engage in.

2. **Regularity:** the predictability of your bodily functions and routines, such as sleeping or elimination.

3. **Initial Response to New Situations:** your comfort with unfamiliar situations, people, or experiences.

4. **Adaptability:** your general comfort level with change of any kind.

5. **Predominant Mood:** your tendency to see the glass half full or half empty.

6. **Persistence:** once engaged, how easily you can let go of activities, feelings, or having your way.

7. **Perceptiveness/Distractibility:** how much you are distracted by what you notice or hear around you.

8. **Intensity:** the depth or level of emotional reaction you have to experiences.

9. **Sensitivity:** the degree of awareness or reaction you have to sensory stimuli (auditory, visual, tactile, etc.), and how much or little it takes for you to notice.

Their work proved important in three significant ways. First, it scientifically established that you are born with a unique pattern of behaviors. Second, it provided a framework and vocabulary for looking at those behaviors. Third, it established that childhood behavior patterns continued into adulthood.

At last, teachers and other professionals had a way to understand why a particular child acted and reacted as he did. Parents also had a way to understand children's behavior—as well as their own.

When you understand these nine traits, you have a useful new tool that changes the way you relate to yourself and the way you see your children. (Many parents have revelations about their relationships with their children when they look at their individual natures and how they do or don't mesh. Stay tuned for Chapter 5, where we'll delve into this—but don't skip.)

The Impact of Nature

Because temperament is based in neurology and genetics, it doesn't significantly change. It has a lifelong impact on our relationships, decisions, and feelings. Parenting, maturity, and experiences may influence the behaviors, but you cannot expect to outgrow the traits' propensities.

Take Sam. He went from being a kid who couldn't sit still to being an adult who organized the ski club and soccer league while renovating his house—all in his spare time.

Jane, easily distracted by peripheral happenings as a child, became the police officer famous for noticing the almost-missed clue of a crime scene.

Jake, as a child, would eat only hamburgers; Jake the teenager eats a BLT for lunch every day.

TRY THIS: *Think back to your childhood. How did parents or teachers describe you (e.g., bookworm, daydreamer, tomboy, always running ahead, etc.)? Now think of yourself as an adult. Are there similarities? Can you see this childhood characterization of you reflected in your adult behavior patterns?*

Your Nature

Seeing yourself in terms of your temperament can be quite eye-opening. In workshops, the "lightbulb" moments when parents make the connection between their behaviors and temperament traits are great to witness. Suddenly, everyone is sharing memories and stories about a childhood behavior that now makes sense, or the weird reaction they have to certain lights and odors that no one else even notices. We all feel the excitement, relief, and empowerment that come with this understanding. Attitudes begin changing almost immediately. Compassion replaces judgment, and curiosity overrides embarrassment. Many tell us that acquiring this new vocabulary and perspective not only helps them make better choices for themselves, but enhances all their relationships.

SELF-ASSESSMENT—WHAT'S MY NATURE?

Here is a simple self-assessment. Its purpose is to help you map out your temperament along the nine traits.

Below are the nine traits and three ways this trait could manifest itself in your life. Choose one behavior (a, b, or c) that sounds the most like you in each situation.

1. Activity Level: How much physical movement does your body need?

Think about your likely activity level at an all-day neighborhood party with sports, food, dancing, and friends.

a. You are the Energizer Bunny—starting with volleyball and still going strong six hours later on the dance floor.

b. The volleyball was enough for you. After lunch and cleanup, you chat with neighbors. At night you dance a little, but mostly listen to the music.

c. Never mind the running and sweating. Good conversation, good food, and a game of horseshoes make it a great day. You're home reading when the dancing starts.

2. Regularity: How much do you have to keep to a schedule to feel comfortable?

Consider your comfort with irregularity when an unexpected opportunity takes you on a dream trip to India.

a. Enthusiasm quickly turns to irritability when the different time zones throw off your sleep and eating schedule. The foreign food upsets your stomach and the scarcity of public toilets prevents regular elimination.

b. It takes a couple of days to get over the jet lag and the early dinner hour, but then you adjust. Your digestive system never quite gets used to all the curries, but you mostly enjoy the cuisine.

c. You have flexible routines, so travel is rarely a problem. Your body quickly adjusts to the time and schedule changes. Your favorite part is exploring remote villages and trying out the local cuisine.

3. Initial Response to New Situations: How do you approach new experiences/ideas?

You decide to take a course on web design at the local community college. How will you react on your first day?

a. You find out all you can about the class before the first session, needing to know what to expect to assuage your anxiety about this new experience. On that big day you get there early, sit in the back, and quietly take in the scene.

b. The first session you take copious notes but store up all of your questions for an opportunity to ask someone you know at a later time. You chat with the people around you and begin to settle in.

c. An active participant from the moment you walk in, you take the opportunity to ask all your questions and share your ideas. You collect names and email addresses of fellow students.

4. Adaptability: How easily do you adjust to change?

The family is growing and you must make a decision about expanding the house you have or moving to a larger home. How does your comfort with change impact your decision?

a. You like things just the way they are, so you have trouble admitting that a bigger house is needed. When your spouse finally convinces you, renovation feels like the only comfortable choice. The idea of moving to a new house and neighborhood far from friends feels totally overwhelming and undesirable.

b. You have little difficulty with small changes, but major life changes are never easy. You see the need for a larger home. Despite your discomfort, you weigh the factors that make moving or renovation a better choice and go with the one that makes the most sense.

c. Change does not create discomfort as much as excitement. You love the idea of starting over with a new home and new experiences. Anxious to get things rolling, you call the realtor immediately.

5. Predominant Mood: Do you tend to be more optimistic or pessimistic?

You've read the public health recommendations about getting the flu vaccine. How might your outlook affect your decision?

a. Of course you will get the flu shot. In fact, you call the doctor to schedule the earliest possible appointment for your whole family, just in case he runs out of vaccine.

b. You get your doctor's advice, think on it for a few days, and then decide *better safe than sorry*. You'll schedule an appointment before winter.

c. You see no reason. You're healthy. If you should get sick you'll get better, so you have nothing to worry about.

6. Persistence: How much determination do you bring to activities and decisions?

How determined do you remain when the "easy to assemble" swing set turns out to be less than easy?

a. Your determination never wavers in the face of frustration. You pass on dinner and work late into the night despite pleas from your spouse to leave it for tomorrow or get help.

b. You start out determined, figuring it will take an hour, tops. After two frustrating hours you concede being in over your head and ask your handyman neighbor for help.

c. You feel like screaming fifteen minutes into the project. You give it another ten minutes before throwing your hands up in surrender. You return it to the store.

7. Perceptiveness/Distractibility: How much are you distracted by things around you?

While cleaning the garage, how focused do you remain?

a. It takes twice as long as it should, what with the kids fighting in the sandbox, the weeds choking the tulips in the garden, and the break to take the dogs for a walk after you heard them whining in the house.

b. Your garage gets cleaned up with a minimum of distractions. You pull out a weed or two while admiring the tulips, and you hardly register the kids fighting or the dogs whimpering inside.

c. You win the prize for Least Distracted. When you are focused on a task, you notice or hear little else. Your spouse swears the place could burn down and you would probably not realize.

8. Intensity of Feelings and Reactions: How reserved or expressive are you?

At a Little League game, what kind of spectator are you?

a. You cheer and shout till you are hoarse. More than once folks around you have to remind you to sit down as you constantly pop out of the bleachers and annoy the umpire.

b. You sit and watch, cheering when your son's team makes a good play, even standing when the play gets exciting.

c. Your quiet demeanor and reserved cheers may not seem enthusiastic, but you wouldn't miss his game for anything.

9. Sensitivity: How much are you affected by sensory stimulus?

How much stimulus can you handle on the third-grade field trip that includes a long bus ride with the kids?

> a. Your headache starts before you ever reach the museum. First there was the confusion and noise getting thirty kids on the bus. Then the singing and harsh lights on the bus continue to stoke your discomfort.

> b. What a relief when you finally got the kids in their seats. It took a while, but now you can lie back, tune out the singing, and read the newspaper.

> c. The confusion and noise don't bother you in the least. On the bus, you join the kids singing and even manage a nap. You arrive at the museum refreshed.

Be sure to keep your responses. You will be using them in a later chapter, which promises to be very interesting.

For now, if you had any strong feelings while completing this self-assessment, jot them down in the "My Notes and Questions" area at the end of this chapter. Then read on.

Accepting What Is

Perhaps while taking the above self-assessment you were reluctant to admit a particular truth about your temperament. You may have been thinking, "Oh! I am much too loud and boisterous," or "I'm so bad at keeping to a schedule, it's amazing my family functions at all." When the expression of a temperament trait seems to have too much intensity, or not enough, you may find it hard to accept that aspect of yourself. There might also be a tendency to judge it as bad, wrong, or difficult because others have—especially parents and teachers when you were growing up. It can be helpful, as you fight these inner critics, to remember the following facts:

- What you are born with, your individual nature, cannot be right or wrong, good or bad.

- Everything is subjective. One person's "difficult" is another person's "spirited"; "boring" to one person may feel "balanced or centered" to another.

- Every expression of a temperament trait has inherent strengths and challenges. The "drama queen" may tend to overreact, but she will also know expansive joy; the "fuss budget," who is irritated by the slightest noise or an uncomfortable fabric, gets to experience the gentle sea breeze or the call of the bobwhite that others miss.

- You're not the only one with this behavior.

Acceptance is a great life tool, and it is an *essential* parenting tool for seeing your child and having him feel "acceptable" and loved. As a parent, accepting your temperament is the first step to seeing and accepting your child's temperament. When you respect and accept your nature, it provides a model for your child and gives him permission to do the same. So, replace those harsh judgments and self-critical statements with the mantra:

There is no right way or wrong way—it's just the way I am!

SELF-ASSESSMENT—DESCRIBING YOUR NATURE.

A downloadable version of this self-assessment is at www.parentinginyourownvoice.com.

The purpose of this self-assessment is to spell out, objectively, what you have learned about your individual temperament.

Next to each temperament trait, write a nonjudgmental, declarative statement describing this trait in you.

For example: 1. Activity Level: I have a lot of energy, which makes it difficult for me to sit still for long periods of time and easy for me to run around with the kids at the playground and take a Zumba class in the evening.

1. Activity Level (need for physical movement) _____

_____

_____

_____

2. Regularity (of biological functions: sleeping, eating, and elimination; or habitual routines) _____

_____

_____

3. Initial Response to New Situations (comfort with unfamiliar situations or experiences) _____

_____

_____

4. Adaptability (comfort level with change of any kind) _____

_____

_____

_____

5. Predominant Mood (perceiving the glass as half full or half empty) ___

_____

_____

_____

6. Persistence (the ability to let go of activities, feelings, or having your way)_____

_____

_____

_____

7. Perceptiveness/Distractibility (how much you notice or hear around you) _____

_____

_____

8. Intensity (degree of reaction) _____

_____

_____

9. Sensitivity (degree of awareness or reaction to sensory stimuli: sound, touch, smells, etc.)_____

_____

_____

As you continue this chapter, come back to these statements and add any new insights you gain about your nature.

Understanding "Why"

Now that you have words to describe your individual tempo, behaviors, and reactions, life becomes clearer and easier. Your choices for yourself take on new relevance, giving you permission to ask for what you need and to create environments that work for you. What you used to feel self-conscious about you can now make sense of and accept as part of your unique nature. Suddenly you understand why regular schedules support or stifle you, why you get more distracted than your partner does, or why people call you Eeyore.

Examples of people who discovered "whys" for their behavior:

Rita never liked big parties. She loves people, has many close friends, and hates to be alone; nevertheless, she avoids large social gatherings. Learning about temperament helped her to realize that it wasn't parties she hated, but the initial experience of walking into them. Her first reaction to new experiences is anxiety.

Mark stopped calling himself obsessive when he learned that his strong drive to complete a task before moving on to something else was shared by many people with a high degree of persistence in their nature.

Wendell has more compassion for himself now that he understands his tendency to frame things in a pessimistic light. Instead of feeling like a doom-and-gloom guy, he acknowledges that, like Woody Allen, he is sensitive and often fretful that bad things, such as car accidents or catching a cold, will happen to him and his loved ones.

Our very own Joan has always viewed herself as undisciplined and disorganized. She eats, works, and sleeps at different times on different days, often criticizing herself for lack of a daily routine. Seeing herself in terms of the temperament trait of "Regularity," she realizes that her variable schedule is right for her. Being irregular is in her nature and not a sign of a character flaw.

TRY THIS: *Is there a behavior you've always wished were different or just one that frustrates or confuses you? Can you link it to a temperament trait? Write about it here.*

_____

_____

_____

_____

_____

Making Accommodations

With understanding and acceptance of our natures, we have the opportunity to make changes in our lives to accommodate our natural rhythms and reactions. Accommodations can take many forms—from creating simple routines for eating and sleeping, to strategically scheduling exercise classes, to making a total lifestyle change regarding when and where we live or work. Arranging your life to be compatible with your nature and working with your nature to be compatible with your life can bring ease and flow to your days.

Here are some examples of accommodations and strategies that Rita, Mark, and the others cited above have created for themselves:

Rita, who learned that she likes parties but needs time to acclimate to new people and situations, now understands and allows herself time to breathe through initial uncomfortable feelings. She has learned that very soon they subside and she can have fun.

Persistent-natured Mark has not only learned to appreciate the value of being a "finisher," but understands that giving himself specific limits helps keep his tendency to get over-involved in check.

And Wendell, who tends to view the glass as half empty, can now remember to get a little distance from his feelings, laugh at himself a bit more, and sometimes even acknowledge that it's his temperament that accounts for his anxiety, not the "truth" of the situation.

It's been helpful for Joan to stop judging herself and be more accepting of her nature. And she has developed a few strategies that help her to be more organized, such as setting some parameters around when to go to sleep and wake up. When there's a lot on her plate, she makes a schedule for the activities for the next day that serves as a guide, allowing for the flexibility she needs while ensuring that everything gets addressed.

EXERCISE: ACCOMMODATING YOUR NATURE.

The purpose of this exercise is to consider your nature and make realistic accommodations in your life. Return to the above nine statements you wrote about your temperament (pages 32–34). Read each statement and consider any shifts or changes you can make in your present life to accommodate this aspect of your nature. If it's helpful, use the questions below to consider ways to accommodate your nature.

- How much physical activity feels best? How can I make time for it?

- Is my work and chores schedule in sync with my rhythms of eating and sleeping?

- Do I allow myself the time I need to experience and process my emotional reactions?

- Do I resist change at all costs? Have I found a way that makes it easier for me to cope? Does breaking it down into smaller steps help?

- Am I aware of whether I tend to see the cup half empty or half full or in between?

- What work schedule suits me best? Keep at it until I'm finished, short intervals with varied tasks, or other ways?

- In what conditions do I work best? Alone in a quiet room, or with music blaring? How can I create a setting conducive to my work style?

- Do I take a breath and think before reacting explosively? Can I explain to people that being low-key or super enthusiastic is simply my style—and not to be put off by it?

- Am I overwhelmed in places like the mall, where my senses are bombarded? Have I found ways to protect my eyes, ears, skin, etc. from being overloaded by sensation? Can I consider typical daily activities and ways to modulate the amount of stimuli I have to handle?

Stretching Beyond Your Nature

Sometimes our temperaments don't fit very well with our environment or our circumstances, and a trait creates problems or limitations for us. When this occurs, we may have to step out of our comfort zone and adopt behaviors that aren't so easy, given our nature. For instance, Peggy, a highly active person, has a 9-to-5 desk job. While it is certainly possible to make accommodations for the trait, such as changing jobs, often this is not possible or even desirable. Formulating ways to stretch ourselves beyond a limiting aspect of our nature creates more wiggle room so we don't feel confined or hampered by our own temperament.

For Peggy, perhaps exercising vigorously each morning and evening and then striving to extend the amount of time she can stay seated a little each day could help her. Or she could find ways to do more work out of her chair, such as answering phone calls or reading standing up.

Another example is David. A loving, responsible father and partner, David is not very persistent. When the toilet leaked or the garage door wouldn't open, after a few moments of frustration he simply gave up and moved on. As a result, there were lots of unfinished projects in the house and yard. Besides being a source of constant friction in his family relationships, his lack of persistence frustrated David. His difficulty staying with meaningful challenges got in the way of things like improving his guitar playing through lessons and extended practice. So, along with accommodations, like having phone numbers of the local plumber and allowing himself short spurts of musical expression, David worked each day to extend his ability to attend and persevere a little beyond his natural limit. He tried to stay with a project or a song five minutes more, then ten, working to expand his tolerance beyond what felt natural.

Though you can't completely change it, if you are accepting and realistic, you can work to stretch and grow aspects of your temperament that feel limiting to you.

> **TRY THIS:** *If there is a trait you feel you want to expand, and not merely accommodate, list here one or two ideas to help you to stretch this limiting aspect of your nature. Remember to do so with acceptance and compassion as well as oomph!*
>
> _____
>
> _____
>
> _____
>
> _____
>
> _____
>
> _____
>
> _____

In much the same way that listening to your voice can direct your decisions, understanding and accepting your unique nature can provide insight into your behaviors and needs. Empowered with this understanding and acceptance, you can now practice bringing out your strengths, getting support for your struggles, and creating the life rhythms that best serve you. You also have a new vocabulary—a fresh way to communicate your needs to those you live with or work with. Sharing this self-knowledge and being aware of each other's natures lessens conflict and invites mutual respect and support.

CHAPTER *2* TAKE-AWAYS

- *You are born with a temperament or nature. It has a lifelong impact.*

- *Every individual has a unique pattern of temperament traits.*

- *The way you express those traits is not set in stone. It is influenced by parenting, maturity, and life experiences.*

- *No expression of a trait is inherently bad or good.*

- *There are strengths and struggles that come with every aspect of one's nature.*

- *Acceptance of your individual nature is self-loving and productive.*

- *Knowing and accepting your nature allows you to work with it and make accommodations for it throughout your life.*

- *Whenever possible, consider and account for your temperament when making choices in your life, from daily routines to vacation travel.*

- *While we can't completely change our nature, we can work to stretch aspects of a trait that feel limiting.*

- *Parents who know and accept their own nature will be better able to respect and value their child's individual temperament.*

My Notes and Questions

3

Your Values

Our voice helps us express our truth as our temperament colors who we are. Now we turn the spotlight on our values. Values reflect our principles and the things we cherish and believe in. They represent what is important and meaningful to us, which evolves and changes throughout our lives. Personal values are different from cultural values, moral values, or the family values we hear about from politicians. Family, culture, life circumstances, and life experiences all influence our values. But when filtered through our voice—that is, when our values come into alignment with what our voice tells us is right—values become personal, powerful, and true for each of us.

Whether you are aware of them or not, your values influence your feelings, actions, and decisions, including the deep feeling of discomfort when you act contrary to a value. They infuse your life with integrity, purpose, and pleasure. So, if you haven't given your values much thought lately, here's your chance. With help from the following 3C exercises, you will: **C**larify the values that matter most to you, **C**onnect with them deeply, and **C**ommit to them with a *Quality of Life Statement.* Then we'll share some of our favorite tips for integrating values into everyday life, transforming them into actions, and remaining connected to them during the hustle and bustle of life. When you keep in touch with your values, you know what feels right for you, so you act consistently and make decisions with confidence. As a parent, focusing on your values provides you with a vocabulary and a framework for parenting that helps you to set priorities and calmly stand behind your decisions.

What Are My Personal Values?

Values are made personal by finding the meaning and place they have for you in your life. When you forge an internal connection to a principle, you essentially transform it into a personal ideal. Commitment to that ideal follows naturally once you clearly understand what you hold dear, and why. Because your values change over time and circumstances, it's necessary to periodically revisit them. It's not often you take the time to reflect on what's important to you, so let's begin with a process that helps you Clarify, Connect, and Commit to the values you want to live by. (Joan wants to thank a Farm Beginnings workshop, by LandStewardshipProject.org, which she attended in the early 1990s in Minnesota, for inspiring the following self-assessment.)

SELF-ASSESSMENT—CLARIFY: IDENTIFYING YOUR VALUES.

A downloadable version of these self-assessments is at www.parentinginyourownvoice.com.

The purpose of this five-part self-assessment is to uncover your core personal values.

Directions:

1. In Column A in the tables that follow, write the number that best expresses how satisfied you are with the degree or presence of each value in your life. Write the number next to the value, where: 0 = not at all satisfied; 1 = slightly satisfied; 2 = somewhat satisfied; 3 = moderately satisfied; 4 = considerably satisfied; and 5 = extremely satisfied. (For example, if Creativity is a value you would like to emphasize much more in your life, you might put 1 or 2 to indicate that you are only slightly or somewhat satisfied.)

2. Next, in Column B, for each value identify how concerned you would feel if that value were significantly **reduced** in your life, where: 0 = not at all concerned; 1 = slightly concerned; 2 = somewhat concerned; 3 = moderately concerned; 4 = considerably concerned; 5 = extremely concerned. (For example, if you love beautiful things in your house and their presence were to be significantly reduced in your life, you might rate Aesthetics a 5, extremely concerned.)

3. Column C is where you determine how much happier you would feel, for each value, if it were significantly **increased** in your life, by ranking your feelings: 0 = feeling indifferent; 1 = slightly more happy; 2 = somewhat happier; 3 = moderately happier; 4 = considerably happier; or 5 = happier by an extreme amount. (An example might be that you have little interest in ramping up Adventure in your life, so 0 would indicate that you would be indifferent to having that value increased.)

4. Now, **add the numbers in Columns B and C together** and place the sum in Column D. (Don't do anything with Column A for now.) This score reflects the relative importance of each personal value to you.

5. Circle the five or six personal values that have the highest score in Column D.

PERSONAL VALUES

Don't see a value important to you? Add it at the bottom.
And don't be limited by our descriptors in parentheses.

	A	B	C	D
CREATIVITY (imagination, invention, originality)				
PERSONAL GROWTH (self-knowledge, use of potential)				
COMPETENCY (achieving mastery)				
FAMILY HAPPINESS (good relations with family members)				
INTIMACY (closeness and trust in relationships)				
ECONOMIC SECURITY (personal financial security)				
ADVENTURE (challenge, risk taking, exploration, thrills)				
INDEPENDENCE (self-sufficiency)				
PLEASURE (having fun, sensuality, recreation)				
ORDER (structure, predictability, organized environment)				

PERSONAL VALUES (continued)

Don't see a value important to you? Add it at the bottom.
And don't be limited by our descriptors in parentheses.

	A	B	C	D
COMMUNICATION (expression and listening)				
HUMOR (playfulness, lightheartedness, wit, cleverness)				
POWER (authority, influence, leading)				
INTEGRITY (honesty, courage of convictions, being responsible)				
SERVICE (helping others, advocating, educating)				
SOCIAL ACTIVISM (actively working to change your community and society)				
RECOGNITION (status, respect, admiration)				
AESTHETICS (appreciation of man-made beauty, such as architecture, fashion, and design)				
ARTS (appreciation of art, music, theatre, performance, literature)				
WINNING (competition with others, goal attainment, triumph)				

PERSONAL VALUES (continued) Don't see a value important to you? Add it at the bottom. And don't be limited by our descriptors in parentheses.	A	B	C	D
INTELLECT (pursuit of knowledge and ideas)				
EMOTIONAL INTELLIGENCE (social perceptiveness)				
TRADITION (rituals, cultural heritage)				
ENVIRONMENT (nature, sustainability of resources)				
SECURITY (safety, stability, and well-being for yourself and loved ones)				
SPIRITUALITY/RELIGION (belief in higher power, acceptance of what is)				
HEALTH/ATHLETICISM (physical well-being and body-based activities)				

Good work. You now have five or six values that represent you and what you want in your life. The next step is to make them more than simply a list of words that gets placed in a desk drawer or misplaced in the recesses of your consciousness.

SELF-ASSESSMENT—CONNECT: REFLECTING, PRIORITIZING, WRITING, AND SHARING YOUR VALUES.

The purpose of the second C is to make your list of values more meaningful and memorable. You'll do this with reflection, writing, and sharing. One of the reasons to take the time to do this written exercise is that it deepens your connection to your values.

1. First, check: Do you have a circled value that has a low satisfaction grade (Column A)? If so, think about why that is. Ask yourself, "Is this value really important to me? If it is, why is it not in my life more?"

2. Next, in the spaces below, record your five or six circled values in order of importance, with number one being the most important.

3. Now write a statement about how or why each value is important to you. Not everyone thinks about a value in the same way. This is your opportunity to go inside and explore your own feelings and ideas.

For example: 1. Environment: The fun of outdoor activities and the pleasures of nature are important to me because they help me feel energized, centered, and connected to something bigger than myself.

1. _____

_____

_____

2. _____

_____

_____

3. _____

4. _____

_____

_____

5. _____

_____

_____

6. _____

_____

_____

TRY THIS: *Think of the axiom, "To name them is to claim them." This activity gives your values a voice by declaring them out loud and with conviction—preferably to others. An exercise Sheila did years ago as a workshop participant still resonates. She stood in the center of a circle and wholeheartedly declared a personal goal to each person in the circle. Five repetitions later, she realized that her goal felt different. Her words were now internalized with a new level of conviction and ownership. Do this in your parenting groups, with spouses, family, or friends. You can also try reading your value statements numerous times out loud, just to yourself. Your personal connection and intention will strengthen when you do this. Also, when you declare to others, "This is what is important to me and a part of who I am," you naturally feel more committed—it's like making a promise to yourself.*

SELF-ASSESSMENT—COMMIT: CREATING YOUR QUALITY OF LIFE STATEMENT.

Briefly, a Quality of Life Statement incorporates your core personal values and your five or six statements of why they are important into a personal narrative. This narrative describes your best imagined life. As before, the process of writing connects your words to a sense of ownership or commitment. As you work with the words, shifting emphasis and getting clearer, that ownership deepens. Ultimately, the purpose of this exercise is to integrate these values into your life. When completed, your Quality of Life Statement serves as an inspiration and an accessible reminder of what is most important.

Parents, even skeptical ones, give this exercise a high grade. Designing how to live life according to what's most important often generates excitement and infuses people with a sense of new possibilities. It's as if once they've stated their intention and imagined a life lived in alignment with their personal values, they can't wait to start living it!

To help you get started, Sheila bravely offered to share her process of writing a QLS, with the caveat that this is her process and only offered as an example, not a template.

Here are her values and statements that describe what they mean to her, from the second C exercise:

1. Family Happiness: *the well-being of family members: emotionally, physically, financially, and spiritually. Being available to my children, husband, etc. in any way that I can to support them in actualizing themselves.*

2. Integrity: *Mind, body, spirit. Living in ways that nourish and maintain my wholeness: meditation/reflection, exercise, connection/community.*

3. Environment: *Appreciating and relating to the natural world daily and caring for the living world, personally and on a larger scale, politically.*

4. Intimacy/Communication: *Sharing of myself openly and learning about others, personally and professionally.*

5. Creativity/Aesthetics: *Appreciation of the presence of beauty in nature, people, forms, colors, etc. and seeing and thinking creatively. This includes expressing what that appreciation inspires in me.*

Now, the next step is to integrate these values into a narrative. Sheila explains: "The writing of this statement was very much a process for me. When I first reread the description of each of my five values, I realized a few of them did not ring true, and I revised them. Then, I wrote a heart-felt Quality of Life Statement. However, when I went back and read it, the words did not carry me home to those values. After experimenting, I found that simple straightforward 'trigger words' were more helpful than more eloquently written prose. These are words that instantly connect me to the personal meaning and importance of each value. Using those words, I made my Quality of Life Statement into a series of short statements setting each value apart. Now when I read them, I connect to each individually, giving it more emphasis and clarity for me."

Here is Sheila's most recent Quality of Life Statement:

My life is on track most when I:

- *Am connected and available to my family, close friends, and community, giving of myself, with lines of communication open and flowing.*

- *Tune in to my voice, with clarity and time to reflect, exercise, meditate, and study.*

- *Create and appreciate beauty.*

- *Spend time in nature. Regularly take action to care for our natural world and its inhabitants.*

Before you write your own QLS, a few last thoughts:

- Writing in a quiet, undisturbed environment always supports clarity and focus.

- "Truth" is more likely found in your heart (*feeling* your words) than in your head (*thinking* the words).

- Because this is about visions and ideals, don't concern yourself with practicality and current life circumstances. (You can worry about these later.)

- The values you can envision in your life are the ones you will live.

Using your five or six most important values from page 49–50 as your guide, write your own Quality of Life Statement here.

My Quality of Life Statement

_____

_____

_____

_____

_____

_____

_____

Now, leave this on your desk. Give your feelings and words time to percolate. When you come back to it, ask yourself, How does it resonate? Is this a good format for me? What changes would help? And finally, is this an accurate roadmap of what I want in my life? **Put your Quality of Life Statement in an accessible place and commit to reading it often.**

Change Happens

Perhaps the most remarkable thing about writing down our values like this is that it often serves as a kick in the pants and inspires spontaneous change. Here are stories from individuals who were moved to make a change that honored their values.

Sarah identified the environment as a top value. Every morning while jogging the bike path she fumed about the trash and dog poop. Change happened when she acknowledged to herself that anger wasn't going to improve the environment. Instead, she met with town officials and helped raise money so that trash receptacles and recycling bins were available along the paths. Doggie waste bags were attached to a nearby pole and a polite sign asked folks to clean up after their pets. Soon squads of scouts got involved and followed her example at other public gathering spots. Together they are raising the community's awareness.

Samantha and Jake both put financial security at the top of their individual values lists. They took a workshop on financial investing and started meeting monthly with a small group of friends to learn and discuss matters related to financial planning. They now feel much clearer and more secure when discussing future plans, budgets, and those typically "stressful" topics.

Tradition was a value Lexi wanted more of in her life. The desire moved her to make a beautiful book of her grandmother's special holiday recipes along with family stories of how the holidays had been celebrated through the years. This year the whole family recreated one celebration, and then the children joined Lexi in the kitchen to prepare a favorite recipe. Now she has plans underway to make books for each of the children.

EXERCISE: TRANSFORMING A VALUE INTO AN ACTION.

The purpose of this exercise is to take one small step toward integrating your values into your life by taking action.

The first step is to dream. Identify one thing you would like to do that embodies one of your values. (It can be a big dream, such as putting your value of Social Activism to work to cure world hunger.)

Now, think of one small step you can take in the direction of that goal. (Perhaps you sign up for emails from political groups addressing world hunger, or join an organization like Oxfam, or contribute to your local food bank.) Now really do it!

Living Your Values: Why Is It so Hard?

Congratulations! You have taken a big step to understanding an essential part of who you are. When you make a strong connection with what you believe in, you are apt to feel inspired and ready for change to happen NOW. That's understandable, but not necessarily realistic. Even the best intentions get derailed by life sometimes. We get too busy and forget, or we get distracted and act out of habit. Many of us are uncomfortable with conflict and keep the peace by forgoing our own truth and deferring to someone else's. Other times the desire to please overrides our better judgment—and our values. Whatever your personal obstacles may be, know that they are universal challenges and part of everyone's experience. Some days you will do better than others. The good news is, thanks to your values, you know where you want to go. Now you just need to be mindful that you are on the right road to get there.

> **TRY THIS:** *During the past week or two, think of a time you acted or reacted in a way inconsistent with your values. Why, do you think? Were you too busy or too distracted? Did you perhaps choose to ignore a value because you wanted to avoid discord or displeasing another? Ask yourself this: If I were being observed, what would my actions in that situation say about me and what I think is important?*

A Strategy for Taking the Right Road

As much as we would all like our values to guide us throughout the day, we know it takes a lot more than good intentions. Living our values takes awareness and lots of practice. You know how easy it is to shift into the habitual world of unconscious, distracted responses and knee-jerk reactions. You mindlessly walk into the house and press the flashing answering machine button. Next thing you know you are returning phone calls while putting groceries away and throwing a load of laundry into the dryer. Children have radar for sensing an opportunity. This is the moment they ask to have a friend sleep over on a school night or play video games before homework. Your distracted nod of the head is as good as a "yes."

Here, we offer a useful *proactive* strategy that helps you to be more conscious and attentive. We borrowed this strategy from Steven Covey's bestseller, *The 7 Habits of Highly Effective People*. He explains: There is a moment between any experience or stimulus and your response—a space between action and reaction. That moment is an opportunity to check in.

That moment Covey talks about is where you bring your values into your decision-making process. Let them inform your actions and words. Here's how. Practice making the moment bigger. Actually stop before you respond to a situation or question, and extend the moment by doing nothing. It's fine to tell a colleague you'll get back with an answer, or to tell a child you need a moment before you decide. It is a great time to just breathe. Extending the moment between a situation and a response not only gives you time to call forth your values to guide you, but it also puts space between you and the urgency of others.

Keep practicing and you will get better at being present and considering your values. Your reward will be fewer moments of regret wondering, "What was I thinking?"

> **TRY THIS:** *Practice being proactive vs. reactive. Over the next few days, intentionally stop before you respond to a situation or question, and extend the moment. You can simply say, "This deserves more attention than I have right now," or just pause with a couple of deep breaths. Take the time you need to consider your options and make your best choice.*

Living Your Values and Parenting

By now, you've probably figured out how all these activities around personal values will help you with parenting. As parents, we want to be conscious of the value system representing and guiding us. It is, after all, what our children see. It is how they come to know us and learn what we think is important. Remember the adage "actions speak louder than words"? This is especially true when it comes to values and parenting.

Children are keen observers and miss nothing—even when you don't think they are paying attention. The way to parent more consciously is to consider the messages inherent in your actions and choices. For instance, if you have the housekeeper pick up your son's room, are you saying he does not need to take care of his own things? If you consistently allow dinnertime to be interrupted by phone calls, is the message that time with family is not a priority? If you restrict your daughter's TV, and then spend all your free time watching TV, will she really think reading is more important?

> **TRY THIS:** *This exercise will help you to become conscious of what your actions are communicating, and whether these messages are aligned with your values. Choose a parenting decision you made or an action you took recently. Try not to judge your decision; instead, consider the possible messages you sent. How did that decision reflect—or not reflect—your values? Was that your intended message? If not, what could you do differently next time?*

As life goes zooming by, how often do you really stop to consider what you believe in, how you want to live your life, and what values guide your decisions? Well, now you've done it! Out of this chapter, you have produced a written, concrete set of values, your Quality of Life Statement, that will help you focus your time and energy on high-quality endeavors that are important to you. This great life compass and parenting tool will direct many of your decisions and priorities going forward. When children observe their parents acting in ways that are consistent with their values, it helps them learn who you are and what is important to you. Your conscious connection to your values is the parenting tool that keeps you living what you preach.

CHAPTER 3 TAKE-AWAYS

- *A value reflects what matters most to you.*

- *Awareness of your values helps you integrate them into your everyday life.*

- *Your Quality of Life Statement is your touchstone for remembering the qualities you want in your life.*

- *Children learn about your values from your actions and the way you choose to live.*

- *Parenting is clearer and more consistent when your values guide your decisions.*

- *The moment before an action or choice is your opportunity to pause and consider your best response.*

- *Conscious values lead to conscious decision making. Being conscious of your values helps you be more proactive, and less reactive, in your parenting.*

- *Values change, so check in with yours periodically.*

My Notes and Questions

4

Your Pleasures, Passions, and Pastimes

In Part I, we've worked on listening to our voice, getting to know our individual natures, and understanding our values. And we've seen how focusing on these aspects of ourselves informs our parenting and improves the quality of our lives. Now we turn our attention to a less acknowledged, yet vital aspect of ourselves—things that give us pleasure, make us feel passionate, and offer us an outlet to express our talents. Whether it's a pickup basketball game, an art class, or a quiet, hot bath, these activities replenish our energy, satisfy our spirit, and relax our body. When we nurture our self with gratifying and pleasant experiences, our life has balance and there is more of our self to share with others—including our children.

We can't recall a single workshop we've ever taught where parents didn't complain about having too little time for *themselves*. Parents tell us things like, "I've lost myself," "I don't know who I am anymore," and "I don't even have space to think my own thoughts." Clearly, the challenge to maintain a sense of self is a universal struggle for parents. Without specific ways to energize and nurture our self, parenting can consume our time and energies, leaving us depleted. Of course, being with your child can be fun, rewarding, and fulfilling. But the kind of nurturing we will talk about in this chapter keeps the focus on *you*. The you you were before you became a parent, and the you you are and want to be, besides being a parent. We provide exercises that will help you discover rewarding pastimes and explore creative ways to include them in your life. By dispelling myths about self-sacrifice and distinguishing selfishness from self-care, you will be freer to locate that little corner of *your* world—and claim it! When your own spirit has been expressed and renewed, you naturally have more spark and enthusiasm for the demands of parenting.

The 3Ps—and Why They Matter

The 3Ps—pleasures, passions, and pastimes—are a lot like child's play. They may appear superficial and frivolous, but below the surface, a lot is going on. 3P activities ignite our imagination, nurture our creativity and self-expression, strengthen interpersonal relationships, and deepen our perception and understanding of the world. In fact, new studies on the brain have found that doing "mindless" activities that are unrelated to your productive work life, such as running or doing a Sudoku puzzle, produce neural activity that's conducive to creative problem solving. In other words, they feed your brain.

When we speak of pleasures, passions, and pastimes we mean any sporting activity, hobby, adventuresome pursuit, daydreaming respite, entertainment, or interest that nurtures your well-being and supports who you are. It can be anything—a massage, playing in a rock band, biking, reading, or writing poetry—as long as it pleases and energizes you.

EXERCISE: TAKING A MINI-PAUSE.

This exercise is your start to nourishing your self. There's a saying from a 1960s cigarette commercial describing "the pause that refreshes." It was a great motto, even if it wasn't a great product, so we're going to steal it here. Make a list of three to five refreshing activities that help you pause from your responsibilities or punctuate your day. But here's the catch: They have to be <u>mini</u>-pauses—fifteen minutes or less. Ideas: a bike ride, meditation, having a cup of tea, applying a ten-minute facial mask, reading a magazine, taking a power nap. Now, commit yourself to one pause-that-refreshes today, and one for tomorrow.

Why Is Self-Nurturing so Difficult?

If you had trouble with this last exercise, you are not alone. We live in a culture that views fun as frivolous, industriousness and selflessness as virtues, and self-sacrifice as a cornerstone of parenting, so it is easy to understand why "taking a break" is such a challenge. Many people, especially overly busy parents, have trouble justifying this kind of "luxury." They may even view it as selfish. But we're going to help you see that being a little selfish—that is, focusing 100 percent on you in small doses—is really the same as self-nurturing. It's good for you!

Going against your habits or self-judgments takes conviction. This is where you can draw on the work and ideas from Chapter 1, where you practiced tuning in to your voice. What would your voice tell you now if you sincerely asked, "Do I deserve this?" Reframe your limiting beliefs (*I don't have time,* and *I need to put myself second)* into new beliefs: *Taking me-time replenishes my soul, recharges my energy, and helps me give more and be a better mom/dad to my kids.*

Who Has Time?

When we ask parents, "What have you done for yourself lately?" we mean: What have you done to meet your own needs for renewal or growth? What attention have you given yourself lately? Most often we hear back how little time there is and how many things need to get done. No question, you have to establish priorities when you're a parent, but your own well-being need not always come at the end of the list.

When time is limited and resources are scarce, creative problem solving is helpful. Here are some ideas parents have shared with us:

> *With no money for childcare, Sondrine arranged an exchange with another mother. One morning a week each took care of both girls, leaving the other mom time for herself.*

> *Martin was able to pursue his passion for gardening by building a safe sandbox/activity area for his son in the yard next to the garden. He can keep an eye on Luke and plant away.*

> *Jan was interested in taking a class at a local art school. She put up a sign for other parents of young children to contact her about sharing childcare. Two people called. Together, they interviewed and hired a babysitter. Once a week, for three hours, the sitter watches their three*

toddlers in a nearby room in the school. Jan enjoys the class so much that, after her son is asleep, she sometimes treats herself and works on her drawings.

Alex took his mother-in-law's offer to watch the baby seriously. On Saturday mornings, Nanny has quality time with her granddaughter and Alex has the morning to himself.

Peggy extended her childcare two hours once a week to play tennis after work. She offsets the expense by bringing her lunch to work during the week. She's eating better, getting exercise, and has more energy for the baby when she gets home.

Javier asked his employer for flexible work hours so his stay-at-home wife, Maria, could have time away from Mommy duties two afternoons a week for things other than errands and shopping, and so he could spend alone time with their twins.

For additional motivation to find time for *you*, here is an abbreviated and cautionary tale about self-care.

> *A tree-felling contest between two lumberjacks was well under way, when one woodsman noticed his competitor had stopped to take a rest. A sense of pending victory grew as he continued chopping furiously. But confidence quickly turned to defeat with the thunder of his opponent's tree hitting the ground.*
>
> *"How, when you stopped to rest, could you possibly win?" demanded the loser.*
>
> *"Oh," the winner explained, "I wasn't resting, I was sharpening my axe."*

The time you take to nourish your spirit is never time wasted. A renewed spirit provides energy and optimism. It gives light to your life. Consider it your obligation to yourself to find time, even fifteen minutes before you collapse into bed at night, to do one small thing just for you. Make time by making dates with yourself—and then keep them.

> *Take Connie, a single mom with two toddlers a year apart. She was feeling lonely and isolated until a mom at daycare invited her to join her book club. Her first reaction was, "Oh, I could never do that." But on second thought, she decided to splurge once a month on a babysitter so she could have a night out with "the girls." That book club has become a source of pleasure, friendship, and renewal for her. Now she can't imagine life without it.*

Selfish vs. Self-Care

Most of us have negative associations with the word *selfish*. However, taking care of yourself and paying attention to your own desires does not make you a selfish or self-centered parent or spouse. It's okay to meet the needs of others, but don't forget your own. You wouldn't serve your family dinner and ignore your own need to eat, would you? Well, nourishing your spirit is just as important as nourishing your body. Self-care means letting go of the idea that sacrificing yourself is part of being a good parent. It means, you have to be a little selfish.

⋯⟶ SEVEN REASONS TO BE A LITTLE SELFISH

In case you need a bit more encouragement or convincing, here are seven good reasons to be at least a little selfish:

1. **Makes you healthier.** Our physical and mental well-being are connected. Laughter is good for us. Too much stress makes us sick.

2. **Encourages kids' self-sufficiency.** Children do not benefit from having all their needs met all the time, because manageable doses of frustration help them discover their independence and develop their skills.

3. **Allows your child her individuality.** Parents who have full lives themselves don't need to live vicariously through their children.

4. **Increases self-awareness.** Just as child's play promotes creativity in children, adult "play" opens the door to your creative self-expression. You may discover thoughts and feelings you weren't aware of.

5. **Enriches you and them.** Your enthusiasm and interest in any activity enriches the whole family by exposing them to new experiences and by demonstrating the value and pleasure of pursuing passions and interests.

6. **Makes you more giving.** A happy, renewed parent has more to give.

7. **Models balance and self-care.** What you model will be what your children learn. If you take care of yourself, you give them permission to do the same within their relationships.

You've practiced mini-pauses and brainstormed ways to create time for yourself. Now you're ready to make a bigger commitment to yourself by scheduling "me-time."

TRY THIS: *Decide what activity you want to start with. Perhaps you will choose to expand your mini-pause to more time by yourself in a bath. Or you will choose something new, like an hour in your woodworking shop, a night on the town dancing, a class—whatever feeds you. Now, take out your calendar and schedule it for a specific day and time. Make this date for yourself along with a commitment to keep it.*

What Interests?

Sometimes the problem with finding personal pursuits is not knowing what to pursue. Maybe your work dominates your life, or you have lost touch with what feeds you. Maybe you never knew.

To connect to passions or pastimes, go back to your childhood and think about what got you excited or involved. Remember what you did when there was nothing to do. Think back to people, vacations, class trips, and seminars that were memorable. Call your parents, siblings, and old friends and ask what they remember.

Next, look to other people to expose you to new things. Ask your neighbor if you can help in his garden. Join your partner at the driving range. Take your child's lead doing a craft. Try something new.

If nothing comes of these efforts, try this exercise.

EXERCISE: CHECKING IT OUT AND CHECKING IN.

The purpose of this exercise is to help you find a satisfying pastime.

Read these words: FUN…EXCITING…FULFILLING…ENERGIZING…RELAXING.

Without thinking, write down the first five activities that pop into your mind.

1. _____

2. _____

3. _____

4. _____

5. _____

Now choose one from the list and try it out. Afterwards, take a moment to check in. Was it satisfying? Do you want to do it again? If not, continue this process, going down your list, until you find something that really clicks for you.

Even if nothing on the list pans out, don't give up. Maintain a sense of adventure, stay open to new possibilities, tune in to your voice, and sooner or later you'll discover something that pleases you.

If you still have trouble seeing a reason to take on this extra "something else to do," go back and reread the Seven Reasons to Be a Little Selfish (pages 66–67). Absolutely everyone benefits from self-care and self-expression—especially you!

Once you've reaped the benefits of self-nurturing, you'll want to make sure it stays in your life.

EXERCISE: MAKING SELF-NURTURING A HABIT.

The purpose of this exercise is to practice self-nurturing regularly so that it becomes natural and habitual.

Get out your calendar, e-calendar, or appointment book. Write down one "me-time" activity a week for the next three months. It can be anything that qualifies as being a passion, pastime, or pleasure—preferably something that will be easy to achieve without a major upheaval of your daily routine. The key is to put it in your calendar and commit to doing it every week for the full three months.

The sacrifices and demands of parenting are real, but so is our responsibility to our self. We don't have to lose our sense of self and deny our own happiness and fulfillment to be good parents. In fact, the opposite is true. The more we allow ourselves to flourish and grow, the more we can share our gifts with our children and the world. With self-nurturing integrated into your life as a parent, your sense of wholeness, individuality, and happiness will grow. Return to this chapter whenever you need to be reminded of the importance of self-care, or need a refresher on how to get more of this good stuff into your life.

CHAPTER *4* TAKE-AWAYS

- *The ways you choose to spend your time reflect your individuality.*

- *Your personal pursuits enrich your life, open the door to creativity, and renew your energy.*

- *Play feeds your brain.*

- *Self-care isn't selfish.*

- *Make time for yourself, and everyone around you will benefit.*

My Notes and Questions

_____

_____

_____

_____

_____

_____

_____

_____

_____

_____

_____

_____

_____

_____

_____

_____

_____

_____

_____

_____

_____

_____

_____

_____

_____

_____

Part 2

Who Is My Child?

In Part I, you focused on your self. You gained a sense of your authentic voice, and you learned more about your unique combination of temperament traits, life values, and the activities that enliven your spirit and make you happy. Now in Part II, you'll turn the focus on your child. You'll discover that many of the topics we explore in this part are enhanced by the self-exploration and self-awareness work you did in Part I.

In Chapter 5, we will look at our child through open and inquisitive eyes to see if we can uncover new ways of really *seeing* him—not who we *think* he is or *wish* he were, but who he genuinely is. We call this his "Me." Next, in Chapter 6, we will discover more about our child's nature using the nine-temperament-trait model from Chapter 2. Chapter 7 is an introduction to some fundamentals about child development. While it's a big topic to which we could devote a whole book, you'll learn some basic ideas that may change the way you see and parent your child from this moment forward. Finally, Chapter 8 tackles three subjects that offer fresh ways to think about and know your child—the types of intelligences that are his strong suits, his unique style of learning, and how he expresses his inventiveness, originality, and creativity.

Remember the folktale about the blind men who came upon an elephant and each described it in a completely different way, depending on which way they approached the animal? Part II is all about giving you new, interesting, and helpful angles from which to view and think about your child, resulting in a richly detailed and multi-dimensional picture of this young being. We'll help you formalize these insights into four statements, which will become building blocks for the customized parenting plan you'll assemble in Part III.

5

Seeing Your Child,
Discovering His "Me"

Part I was designed to help you focus on who you are, in order to gain insights and appreciation for your own individuality. Seeing our self is a necessary first step to seeing our child as an individual. *Seeing* our child means we take an objective stance and then listen and watch with focused attention. We put aside any expectations, prejudices, or fantasies and get to know him as he really is, warts and all! Accurately seeing him matters, because the way we see him greatly influences the way he comes to know and see himself—his "Me." Our child feels valued and accepted when we take the time to know him and respond without judgment, projection, or disappointment.

The journey to discovering your child's *Me* begins with understanding how she comes to know herself and the implications this has for her entire life. Once you appreciate the importance of your child feeling seen, you will also realize that seeing another person fully and objectively isn't easy or automatic. To aid you in the practice, we highlight three skills: self-awareness, listening, and observation. Using these tools helps you make a clear distinction between her and you, discover who she is, and set her on a course for a happy, promising future.

How a Child Comes to Know Her *Me*

Mirrored in your eyes, your child discovers herself. From the beginning, you are her world and most important reference point. By taking in your feelings and reactions, such as the tone of your voice and your response to her cries, your child starts to develop a sense of self. As she grows, she continues to learn about herself through your insight and reflection. How she comes to feel about herself is colored by your emotions and reactions to her. When you appreciate a characteristic of hers, her connection to that part of herself strengthens. Likewise, she may come to feel shame or disconnection from an aspect of herself that emerges when she experiences rejection or harsh criticism. As she develops and her world expands, significant people outside of her family influence her sense of self. Over time, her own experiences and reflection impact her self-image. Throughout her life, as her sense of self continues to develop, these early feelings and ongoing messages support and influence her evolving *Me*.

> *Every Saturday, Sequoia and her dad spent time at the table drawing, cutting, and sculpting. Following her lead, he provided the materials and watched her experiment, appreciating her creativity. Dad was really pleased when he read one of her self-descriptions in the "All About*

Me" booklet she'd made at school: "I like to make things and I am a very creative artist."

In seventh-grade art class Marshal played the class clown, disrupting other students and rarely completing an art project. When his mother asked him about this, Marshal vividly recalled the humiliation he felt when his second-grade art teacher regularly, and all too publicly, made fun of his artwork.

Four-year-old Ben looked in the mirror, pointed, and declared, "I have brown eyes like Mommy's, curly hair like Aunt Chrystal's, my nose is like Grampa's nose, and—" with a large grin—"I have Benny's smile."

When you purposefully work to *see* a child, you validate her Me.

Helping Children Feel Seen

It's one thing to feel that you really do "get" who your child is, but quite another to let him know that you do. Children have a sense of being seen when:

- You listen to them.

- You respond to their needs.

- You acknowledge their feelings.

- You encourage them to tune in to their feelings.

- You confirm your guesses about how they feel by asking them.

- You encourage and value their unique voice.

- You recognize and respect them as individuals separate from you.

- You have realistic expectations for them.

- You verbally acknowledge their efforts and struggles.

- You communicate appreciation for their efforts and acceptance for both their achievements and their failures.

Benefits of Being Seen

Being understood, accepted, and respected—or *seen*—allows your child to feel happy and comfortable with himself. It meets his basic needs to feel valued and worthy of love, and supports his budding voice.

> One parent reported: "My son's face glowed when he noticed me watching him build with Legos. He sat taller as he turned back to his constructing. All I did was stand quietly and watch, silently appreciating his inventiveness. Guess he felt it."

For a child, this experience of being seen lays the foundation for a realistic, confident, and accepting sense of Me. A child's self-esteem is fostered when he is seen.

> By sixteen, Tallulah, a bright, social teen and avid cyclist, independently began her search for a job. Aware of her skills, interests, and desired wage (she wanted to save money for a trip), she set out. Through her two-week search, she handled the rejections reasonably well, discussed strategies with her folks, and finally landed a position as shop clerk in the local bike and sporting goods shop.

The child who feels good about himself is more likely to step outside his comfort level, have better resources for self-control, and have respect and compassion for others.

> During fifth-grade gym class, Joe picked Bill early on for his soccer team, even though Bill was not one of the better players (and was often last to be chosen). The gym teacher saw Bill's look of appreciation

and relief, and saw that Joe noticed it too. It was clear to the teacher, who related this story to the parents, that Joe felt good about including Bill and wasn't overly concerned about winning or popularity.

Tools for Seeing Your Child

Seeing our children is a gesture of love and a commitment to their future well-being; its importance cannot be overstated. The resulting self-confidence, self-acceptance, and sense of competence our children develop will influence the quality of their entire life. While there are many ways we help children feel seen, three tools are particularly useful: **self-awareness, listening,** and **observation.** When we hone these three skills, we are more likely to see our child as she is and value what we see. Once we get good at separating ourselves from our child, paying attention to what she says, and observing her objectively, we will have acquired a priceless set of parenting tools.

The First Tool: Self-Awareness

Self-awareness is something you practiced throughout Part I. Everything you learned about yourself helps you *see* better as a parent. Here, however, we're shifting the focus just a little. Now we want you to see and think about yourself *in relationship to your child.* It is self-awareness that helps keep your identity and your child's identity separate, and awareness that helps you notice how and when you lose sight of your and your child's two distinct selves. The better you get at anticipating and recognizing these next parenting challenges, the more clearly your child will come into view.

Discern your feelings and desires from your child's feelings and desires. The relationship we have with our child is unique. The emotional and physical dependency in infancy binds us in such a way that children seem part of us. Then, the slow process of individuation begins. Our child grows more distinct and independent from us as her individual identity emerges. In our head we acknowledge, even celebrate, our child's independence and individuality, but the relationship is often more complex. We know she is her own person, but somewhere deep inside we still experience her as part of us. When we are alert, we catch ourselves losing sight of her individuality and separateness from us.

> *Throughout her life, Sheila remembers her mom saying some variation of, "Sheila, I'm cold—put a sweater on." This was her humorous and open acknowledgment that it was sometimes hard to separate how she was feeling from the way Sheila felt.*

Acknowledge the hopes, dreams, and preconceptions you may have brought to parenting. Knowingly and unknowingly, we bring opinions, fantasies, expectations, and projections into the nursery with our babies. We have "thought balloons" of sweetly dressed children or articulate little dinner companions, strong feelings about the way she will be or he should behave, visions of proud moments or shared experiences far in the future— you get the idea. As harmless as many of these may be, the danger exists for the child we dreamed, or still dream about, to obscure the child we have. Pay attention to feelings of extreme disappointment or upset related to your child. Ask yourself why you feel this way. When we identify and connect with our preconceived notions and current ideas about how our child should be, these fantasies and expectations lose some of their hidden energy. Then we are free to see and appreciate our child as he is, with his own unique abilities and ways.

Patrice, a journalist, looked forward to the time her daughter, Jackie, would be old enough to talk about world events and relevant political issues. As Jackie matured, it became evident she wasn't the slightest bit interested in the news or political discourse. Patrice struggled with her disappointment and wondered if Jackie might be less intelligent than she hoped. Each attempt to educate Jackie and engage her interest in world events fell flat. Once Patrice stepped back enough to see her daughter from a distance, she noticed for the first time Jackie's appreciation of design and architecture and most things visual. Instead of the fantasized political conversations she might have had with Jackie, Patrice found she enjoyed the excitement of sharing ideas about the world with her daughter through explorations of its buildings and art.

TRY THIS: *Write as many before-baby fantasies and expectations as you can remember. Have fun, don't judge yourself, and really try to go back there. Next, make another list of the ones that snuck up on you later—like when your six-year-old future feminist wanted to be a princess for Halloween, or your teenage son did an instant thumbs down at the mention of your college alma mater. Keep this list handy and add to it as you make new discoveries. This can also be an eye-opening activity to do with a coparent.*

_____

_____

_____

_____

Acknowledge your nature and the experiences that influence the eyes you see through. Sometimes we see our children through eyes that reflect *our* nature and life experiences, distorting what's before us. It may be that we see through a lens that's colored by a lifelong underlying theme, such as competitiveness or distrust. Or we find ourselves in the middle of a situation that triggers an old feeling like insecurity or shame. Maybe we see life through the eyes of a person resistant to new experiences. When the lens we see through is colored or distorted in some way, we stop seeing our children as they are. We all do this to some extent, but when we can learn to catch ourselves, it's like putting on clear glasses with the right prescription—our vision is corrected! Only then are we open to seeing our child's Me.

---> SIX TYPES OF "EYES" PARENTS SEE THROUGH

Here are a few of the "uncorrected eyes" parents have caught themselves seeing through.

1. **Scared/worried eyes:** Cindy constantly asked Josh how he was doing at work, how he felt, how others treated him, always alert for potential dangers or slights from others. Cindy came to realize that her consistently anxious eyes failed to see how capable and well regarded her seventeen-year-old son had become.

2. **Suspicious/negative eyes:** Tom frequently fretted that his young son was too trusting. When he became more aware of the suspicious eyes he often saw the world through, he could appreciate that Jordan was a great judge of people.

3. **Evaluating/judging eyes:** Sally described watching Stephanie play with her friend, feeling pangs of concern and annoyance that she let others direct the play and was not assertive enough. When Sally owned up to the fact that her own lack of assertiveness was the basis for the judging eyes she saw Stephanie through, she was able to see the beauty of her daughter's easy-going and cooperative nature.

4. **Competitive/gloating eyes:** Piano recitals were unpleasant for Steven. His daughter Claire was not nearly as good as some of the others, despite weekly

instruction and daily practice. His competitive eyes actually reflected his own disappointments about not making it as a professional musician. This insight freed Steven, and now he could applaud Claire's hard work and share in their common love of music.

5. **Can-do-nothing-wrong/blinder eyes:** Parents often complained to Jean that her son Peter was aggressive and inappropriate. Each time, Jean dismissed the complaint with a "boys will be boys" remark or a suggestion that another child had provoked him. Jean needed to feel good about herself, and her son was part of that feeling good. When she became aware of her blinder eyes, Peter received the help he needed to manage his feelings and take responsibility for his actions.

6. **Embarrassed/frustrated eyes:** Much to Kathy's dismay, her daughter Blair behaved like a terror on the class trip. Kathy responded harshly and publicly. Her embarrassed eyes kept her from seeing that Blair needed help dealing with having to share Mom. The crushed look on Blair's face made Kathy step back and stop reacting to her own feelings.

Don't beat yourself up each time you lose sight of those feelings that obscure your vision of your child. Instead, remember that this is an ongoing challenge for every parent. With these tools and generous doses of self-acceptance and empathy, you will keep seeing more clearly. Congratulate yourself each time insight opens the window to your child's Me, and stay focused on taking in the view.

The Second Tool: Listening

Our words express our ideas and experiences. Through them, we share a part of our self with another. When your child talks and your response reflects that you are present, open, and committed to understanding, you show him you are listening and interested. Being heard in this way communicates value and appreciation, and that builds his self-esteem. It tells your child in a very important way that you see him and want to know who he is.

Practice listening. Listening is a skill that doesn't come naturally to people in current times. In Native American cultures that did not have written language, people could sit and listen to long, elaborate oral histories, and then repeat these to their children. In Shakespeare's day, people would go to the theatre and listen intently to every poetic word, line, and rhyme in a long play. But today, with instant messaging, fast-paced editing on TV and in movies, and the ever-present allure and interruption of our tech toys and tools, our brains are used to collecting quick impressions and then moving on. As parents, we have to relearn how to quiet our busy minds and eliminate distractions so we can practice listening to our children. No one can be a good listener all the time, so it's helpful to create and capitalize on opportunities to listen to your child.

---> FIVE GREAT LISTENING OPPORTUNITIES

Here are some good opportunities to unplug and practice listening:

1. **After school:** When he comes home from school, and before you tell him to do his homework or practice the piano, pour a cup of cocoa and listen.

2. **Car rides and walks:** Going to and from places is often a time when children talk. Make a point of using these times to listen.

3. **Mealtime:** The dinner table is a place where family members can regularly practice listening to one another, modeled of course, by parents.

4. **After a shared experience:** After watching a movie or attending a party, for example, talk together about what you observed, and about the feelings and reactions you had. Here's an opportunity to listen and learn about one another.

5. **At bedtime:** For whatever reason, children and even teens often open up and reveal all kinds of secrets and inner thoughts after they're tucked in and under the covers.

Keep them talking. Sensitive to our reactions, some children shut down at the slightest sign that we are judging, misinterpreting, or ignoring their words. Without realizing, we can easily slip into teaching, correcting, and assuming—when we want to be listening instead. Keep them talking with these listening strategies and reminders.

---> NINE WAYS TO LISTEN

1. Avoid correcting your child's grammar or word usage when they speak to you. Listen to what they are saying rather than how they are saying it, and wait until later to teach them proper English.

2. When your child talks to you, ask questions for clarity, and avoid grilling.

3. Resist the urge to say something. It often serves to interrupt rather than encourage more communication.

4. If your child isn't chatty, instead of asking lots of questions, tell them something about your day and listen to their response.

5. Alternatively, present a situation that has happened to you and ask for their ideas about ways to handle it.

6. Communicate back to your child what you heard them say. From time to time, this insures that you understand them, and it expresses your interest in getting it right.

7. Accept their corrections without getting defensive.

8. If they are annoyed at something you missed or misunderstood, accept their reaction and understand that it comes from a strong desire for you to hear them and know them. This is a tribute to your parenting. They haven't given up on you or themselves.

9. When you realize you weren't listening, fess up. Explain that you were distracted, and then make a time to talk when you aren't.

Even with our awareness and intention to listen, the many intrusions and distractions in our busy lives continue to challenge our ability to do so. Here are some little "red flags" to use as signs to stop and refocus.

You know you are **not** truly listening when you find yourself:

- Anticipating what they will say next.

- Completing their sentences.

- Multitasking, such as checking your email while your child is talking to you.

- Feeling impatient.

The Third Tool: Observation

Observation is the tool that helps you see your child with fresh eyes and opens you to new discoveries about him. We borrowed it from teachers and psychologists who use it in their work every day when they want to learn more about a child. The key to observation is objectivity. To see objectively you must quiet preconceived ideas, disconnect from expectations and judgments, and become conscious of possible projections. Like a fly on the wall, watch, unobtrusively, without participation or interference. It is unusual for parents to play the role of neutral silent observer, but you will soon discover it is an effective tool you can use often—and gain rich insights.

Joan offered a story from her professional practice about the value of seeing objectively. Good or bad, we tend to see what we expect to see. Her positive expectations and assumptions influenced the way she saw a child she knew well.

> *"I was asked to evaluate a child I had watched grow up. Rebecca was bright, likable, social, and advantaged—the kid most likely to sail through school. The problem was, she was nearing the end of first grade and stood out as one of the slowest readers in her class. It only took one observation of her in this setting for me to find a likely yet unexpected explanation. When I observed with a neutral and professional eye, it was apparent that Rebecca's expressive language was quite delayed in comparison with that of her classmates and was surprisingly weak given her language-rich home environment. It was only by observing through the objective 'eyes of a stranger' that I was able to see what had always been there."*

How Observation Helps Us *See*

Before you practice observing, it's useful to understand when to use observation and why it's such a good tool for seeing your child.

- **Observation helps you know your child better as an individual.** Insight into your child's individual strengths, challenges, interests, and behaviors becomes more evident.

  Observing ten-year-old Kwame struggle making a card for a sick classmate alerted his dad to the fact that he had trouble using scissors.

- **Observation gives you insight into your child's feelings.** Body language, facial expressions, the feeling tone of her words, behaviors, or even play themes can help you understand your child's feelings and experience more deeply. (Although, you won't know for sure until you check in and ask her if you got it right.)

Frank observed Dana as she talked about school with her mother. At every opportunity she inserted a story about how funny or smart the new boy was in physics class. Each time, her face would brighten and she would get more animated as she relayed the story. Later, Frank asked if she was interested in dating the boy. She shyly smiled and asked, "How did you know?"

- **Observation gives you insight into what's on your child's mind.** Discussion topics they initiate, play themes, activities, and areas they focus their energies on often reflect what is going on in their world and their mind. It is how they work through understanding and integration.

  Three-year-old Terry often created a play scene with her dolls where one baby was "bad" and had to be punished. Observing this repeated theme gave her mother insight into feelings Terry was trying to work out. The mom's first reaction was to feel responsible and look at her own parenting. With help she came to realize that her daughter's play-acting was Terry's own interesting way of making sense of good and bad.

- **Observation helps you clarify your understanding of your child.** When you need more information in a specific area, or you want a question answered, observing is a great tool.

  Noticing Bobby's clumsiness, Bobby's dad decided to pay attention to his other motor skills. Bobby also played badminton poorly and didn't like to ride his bike because he wasn't very good at it. Based on these observations, the dad decided to consult a physical therapist.

- **Observation helps you get an accurate picture of how capable your child is.** When you step back and observe what your child does independently, you can better support his independence and set realistic expectations for him.

  Cheryl observed Harry at his friend Graham's house. When Graham suggested they go outside, Cheryl watched as Harry put his jacket on in a flash, along with his shoes (though on the wrong feet). She was thrilled. She hadn't realized Harry could put on his own coat and made a mental note to teach him the trick for matching each shoe to the correct foot.

- **Observation provides opportunities to discover repeated themes or patterns.** After doing a few observations, you may begin to notice patterns of feelings, interests, abilities, behaviors, or ways of relating that repeat in different situations or similar circumstances. The patterns might reflect anything from a temperament trait, to an emotional difficulty, to a strong passion. When you are able to identify these patterns, you have a deeper understanding that supports your child's well-being and sense of being seen.

  Michael enjoyed learning about a variety of things, including bugs, trucks, how our bodies work, and drawing cartoons. After three or four observations, his dad saw a pattern beginning to emerge. Michael sang about everything: about the bugs as he watched them, about his esophagus. He was always singing out his thoughts and discoveries, and doodling on the piano. His dad had never connected this behavior with his ability to play a simple tune on the piano shortly after hearing it. His propensity for music became more and more evident.

···→ NINE OBSERVATION GUIDELINES

Here is a list adapted from the guidelines professionals use to make certain they are being neutral, objective, effective observers.

1. **Give it full attention.** Find time, even small periods, when you can devote your full attention.

2. **Be unobtrusive.** Choose times when children will be least influenced by your presence. (Children often act differently when they know they are being watched.)

3. **Avoid multitasking.** Once you commit to the five or ten minutes, patiently stick with the task. Resist the urge to make a quick phone call or be distracted by another diversion—a lot can happen in a missed moment.

4. **Just watch.** No teaching, encouraging, or correcting. Allow the natural flow without saying or doing anything that might influence or change dialogue or behavior.

5. **Write down what you see and hear.** Be specific and descriptive, giving details about body language, facial expressions, the feeling tone of her words, her behavior, play themes, environmental circumstances, sounds, etc. Whenever possible, write as you watch, even if it is just a word or two to jog your memory later.

6. **Describe behavior, don't interpret it.** For example: "Jerry turned red in the face" vs. "Jerry was angry." (Jerry may have felt embarrassed rather than angry.) "Justin yelled, 'Sorry, I did it all wrong again,' in a loud, strong voice with tears welling up in his eyes," vs. "Justin yelled, 'Sorry, I did it all wrong again,' in a defiant voice." (Justin may have felt more frustrated than defiant.)

7. **Try different vantage points.** Observe in different settings, circumstances, and at different times of the day.

8. **Be respectful.** Children want to be *seen,* not necessarily watched. Sometimes they appreciate your interest and sometimes they feel judged or self-conscious. Older children, in particular, can have strong feelings about privacy. When observing a teen, get their okay to be in the room.

9. **Again, BE OBJECTIVE.** Remember the importance self-awareness plays in objectivity. Think about the eyes you see through, and stay alert for expectations, personal feelings, judgments, and experiences that color how you see.

There may be times during your observations when you notice your child is having real struggles. Become aware of your own feelings and then decide if it is appropriate or necessary to intervene.

> *While observing his son playing with another child in the sandbox, Fred noticed the other child grab his son's shovel and throw it, causing sand to fly up near his son's face. Wanting to jump in, Fred realized he felt protective of his son and angry at the other child. He paused a moment and watched. His son rubbed his eyes for a while, looked around, sighed, and began playing with the truck lying next to him. Fred kept watching. The other child looked over at his son, made a hole in the sand for the truck, and for quite a while after, one made tunnels and the other drove the truck through them.*

If a concern arises from your observation and you feel unclear about whether it is projection of your own feelings or a valid concern, start by acknowledging the confusion and giving the concern a name. With it named and out in the open, you can do additional observations, talk with teachers and other caregivers, check in with your voice, and check in with your child.

> **TRY THIS:** *Try out your observation know-how. For at least five to ten minutes in two different situations or circumstances, observe your child. Have your observation guidelines handy. How did it go? Did you notice any difficulties? Were you able to be objective and keep your emotional distance?*

When we embody the open curiosity of the explorer, we witness the subtle shifts of change and the unique influences our child has on his world. This is one of the most profound experiences of being a parent. It's through our intention and efforts to see our child clearly that we will continue to deepen our understanding and help him feel seen.

Throughout Part II, you will be using the three foundational tools of self-awareness, listening, and observation to focus on specific aspects of your child: their temperaments, interests, ways they learn, and more. You'll be gathering information and cultivating skills to use later in constructing and implementing your parenting plan.

CHAPTER 5 TAKE-AWAYS

- *Children learn about themselves through the eyes and feelings of their parents and other significant people in their lives.*

- *A child feels seen when we listen, respond appropriately, appreciate his individuality, and respect his feelings.*

- *Being seen provides the lifelong benefits for your child of self-knowledge and self-esteem.*

- *Self-awareness helps parents separate who they are from who their children are.*

- *We see children when we come to value them as individuals with their own feelings, struggles, and gifts, which are distinct from ours and our fantasies for them.*

- *Our active participation in listening to our child reflects our interest in him and his value.*

- *Observation relies on focused listening and objective seeing, and helps us know our children more fully.*

- *Listening and observing objectively begins with your intention and gets better with practice.*

My Notes and Questions

6

Your Child's Temperament

In Chapter 2, you had a chance to think about your own temperament—how it has influenced your life over the years and how it impacts your choices and preferences today. Perhaps you had some aha moments of understanding or shifts in perspective that allowed acceptance to replace self-criticism or judgment.

Now you have the opportunity to learn about your child in this same way. Parents describe this newfound understanding of their children's temperament as everything from useful to life changing. It will, no doubt, be an important part of your parenting toolkit. Not only will your child's behavior make more sense, but you will naturally make better parenting decisions. By comparing your temperament profiles, you can see how your child's temperament fits with your own and consider the implications that fit and acceptance play in your parenting. Along with your understanding and insights comes an opportunity to teach your child about herself. The guidance and acceptance you lead with will be the model she follows.

Let's review the nine temperament traits:

1. **Activity Level:** the amount of physical movement typically engaged in.

2. **Regularity:** the predictability of body functions, such as sleeping or elimination.

3. **Initial Response to New Situations:** comfort level with new situations, people, or experiences.

4. **Adaptability:** comfort level with change of any kind.

5. **Predominant Mood:** tendency to see the glass half full or half empty.

6. **Persistence:** once engaged, how easy it is to let go of an activity/feeling/having your way.

7. **Perceptiveness/Distractibility:** the ability to focus despite distractions you can see and hear around you.

8. **Intensity:** the depth or level of emotional reaction to experiences.

9. **Sensitivity:** the degree of awareness or reaction to sensory stimuli (auditory, visual, tactile, etc.)

For more complete descriptions of these traits, refer to Appendix 1, page 231.

ASSESSMENT: TAKING YOUR CHILD'S TEMPERAMENT.

A downloadable version of this assessment is at www.parentinginyourownvoice.com.

In this exercise, you will get acquainted with your child's temperament. The concept is similar to what you did in Chapter 2, but the examples for each trait come from parent descriptions of their children's behavior. (In Appendix I, you can find out what strategies each parent used when parenting these children.)

Below are the nine traits, each with (a), (b), and (c) examples of different degrees of expression.

First: Circle the letter that most closely describes your child's degree of that trait.

Next: Use the "Make it personal" lines to write your own description of something your child typically does that reflects his expression of that trait.

For example, for trait number 1, Activity Level, you circled (c). Then you write a description of your son: "John doesn't have much get up and go. He typically wakes up, snuggles on the couch, finds the remote, and watches TV until we get the backhoe to lift him into the bathtub. He'd sit all day if we let him."

1. Activity Level: Refers to the amount of physical movement that is typically exerted by the child. How much energy *needs* to be released?

Circle the letter that best describes your child's level of physical activity.

a. Jackson constantly needs to move. School is extremely challenging because it requires too much quiet sitting. At home, even when he's sitting, he isn't still—some part of his body is always in motion. After school he needs to have a great deal of physical activity or he will be too revved up to fall asleep. He has difficulty sitting still long enough to finish homework carefully, and he has never fallen asleep easily.

b. Whenever something with wheels is available, Troy is riding it, chasing it, or playing with it. At school he can sit and work as long as there is a recess or gym break so he can run and play. After school he likes to have some time to ride his bike or play outside, but then he will come in and do his homework straight through. Before bed there is usually some quiet activity and little drama about going to bed.

c. Lucy seems to be more a thinker than a doer. If you bring a toy to her, she gladly plays with it, but would not likely get it on her own. If she doesn't have a toy, she sits and looks around, takes in her surroundings, or finds something nearby to explore. Even after learning to walk, she preferred to be carried and usually gravitated to the sandbox rather than the slides, swings, or jungle gym. It is also rather amazing how long she can sit in a restaurant without getting antsy.

Make it personal:

_____

_____

_____

2. Regularity: Refers to the degree of predictability that accompanies the child's biological functions.

Circle the letter that best describes your child's level of regularity.

a. Max has always relied on a stable daily rhythm. He's up early, uses the bathroom three times a day like clockwork, and never stays up much past 11. With some adjustments, he can be flexible, but he seems to be at his best within his schedule. (When he was a baby, other parents envied the predictability of our days and nights.) Even now, at fifteen years old, he is looking for those three meals a day at around the same time. Though he goes to sleep a lot later, he still needs his eight hours or he's a cranky mess.

b. Bernadette loves to eat. She goes along with the family's schedule, three meals a day with a midmorning and mid-afternoon snack. Her daily rhythms are fairly regular, but you can't set your watch by her. Sometimes she's asleep by 7, sometimes 8.

c. Fulvia greets each day anew. Some days she's ravenous and can eat throughout the day. Other days she hardly touches a morsel. Nap times and bedtimes are equally different. To have any routine ourselves, we must put her to bed at a certain time and accept that she may stay awake in her room.

Make it personal:

_____

_____

_____

3. Initial Response to New Situations: Refers to the child's response when introduced to a new situation or experience.

Circle the letter that best describes your child's initial reaction to new situations.

a. We were so unsure how to handle Jason in social situations. He's bright and likes people, but when we take him to a party or to the playground, he clings to my leg. He stands there watching for what feels like forever, and then (just around the time to leave) tentatively joins in. He's like that with food, too. We have to offer a new food several times before he'll try it.

b. Francisco really likes to go places and meet new people, but you wouldn't always know it. For example, when a friend's child came running up to him yelling hello while grabbing his hand to show him a game she was excited about, he stopped dead in his tracks and turned to me with a look of desperation on his face. It took a little while for him to warm up to her after that—but he did. The other day we took him to a Japanese restaurant and he had a ball trying the dumplings and tempura dishes. He even tried to use the chopsticks.

c. Melanie has always been a people person. At school, she introduces herself to the new kid or joins the volleyball game on the playground even when she knows no other player. She loves to travel. You could put her in a different bed each night or in a new situation every day and she would be just fine. It's a stark contrast to me, her dad, who feels best staying close to my things and familiar surroundings.

Make it personal:

_____

_____

_____

4. Adaptability: Refers to the amount of time/energy it takes for the child to adjust to change.

Circle the letter that best describes your child's level of adaptability.

a. Shopping for clothes is supposed to be a fun mother-daughter experience. Not for Alyssa and me. She has such a hard time accepting anything new or different. Whether it's a new coat, a new family car, or even a piece of furniture, each experience is met with anger and upset. She'd much rather wear the old coat she's outgrown. Changes are just hard.

b. Wayne takes a little while to switch gears. When we go to his grandparents' house, he needs me there with him for the first hour or so. Then I can leave and he's fine. If we go back the very next day, he still needs me there for a few minutes before he'll say, "Bye, Ma."

c. Nate is so flexible. What a break. Being the youngest of four children, it really helps that he can go with the flow. When I have to run to school for one of his brothers, or take his grandfather to an appointment, he has to be left at a friend's or with a babysitter. If it's a new sitter or I wake him from his nap to take him, he complains for a few minutes, but then he quickly adjusts, and goes with a smile. Nate came into the world like this. We can't take any credit.

Make it personal:

_____

_____

_____

5. Predominant Mood: Refers to the prevalent mood that the child expresses throughout the day—how she views the world in general.

Circle the letter that best describes your child's predominant mood.

a. When my self-esteem was tied to April's responses to me or my attempts to make her smile, I felt quite dejected. Then I stepped back and saw that she responded to everyone and everything similarly. She's very touchy and can be somewhat of a curmudgeon. When other toddlers laugh, she frowns. From her point of view, the glass is usually half empty. Exuberant, gleeful responses? They're just not her way.

b. Hernan gets upset when he's uncomfortable or frustrated. If he hasn't gotten enough sleep and has lots of schoolwork, he may feel sad and burdened and sound a bit like Eeyore. Usually, though, Hernan is cheerful and upbeat. He loves to joke and make his sisters laugh and can brighten everyone's mood.

c. The word *enthusiastic* best describes Dean. Since he was in preschool, he's seemed to find the world to be a very exciting and wonderful place. Of course he gets upset at times, but he doesn't stay upset for very long. He laughs aloud a lot, even if he's reading something funny to himself. His whole being smiles.

Note: It may be difficult to judge a teenager's predominant mood because of the mood swings adolescents typically experience. Go back and think about them as younger children.

Make it personal:

_____

_____

_____

6. Persistence: Refers to the child's ability to let go of an activity or feeling.

Circle the letter that best describes your child's level of persistence.

a. Willie came into the world singing, "I'll do it my way." After running through the labels Oppositional, Defiant, Unreasonable, and Willful, we've come to realize that Focused, capital "F," best describes Willie. Whether he's trying a new sport or a crossword puzzle, he keeps at it. In fact, trying to get him to stop is excruciatingly difficult. When he sets his mind to something, a certain food or pair of sneakers, it's very hard to get him to accept an alternative or take no for an answer.

b. Brielle can concentrate on her schoolwork when it's interesting OR when she has to prepare for a test. If distracted by a phone call or her brother, she can usually get right back to it. If she doesn't understand something, she tends to ask myself or her teacher to explain it to her rather than to go over it and over it until she gets it. When she gets upset about what her boyfriend said or if I set some limit she doesn't like, it's a little difficult for her to let the feelings go. But she still takes care of her responsibilities and doesn't get completely sidetracked.

c. MaryAnn has no stick-to-it-tiveness. Though she may get engrossed in something, in comes her sister or a friend, and she drops everything to join them. If the puzzle or math question becomes challenging, she gives up quickly. She's certainly smart enough to figure things out if she would persevere. On the other hand, she's one who can truly "go with the flow." If plans change, or if she has to settle for a different flavor ice cream, whatever it is, she's accepting and moves on quickly.

Make it personal:

_____

_____

_____

7. Perceptiveness / Distractibility: Refers to the degree the child's focus is interrupted by outside stimuli such as sound, smell, movement, etc.

Circle the letter that best describes your child's focus.

a. Farrell is drawn to everything around him. As he eats his chicken nuggets at the dinner table, he is reaching over to grab his brother's fries. In a flash he might jump up from the table to look for the ambulance he hears down the street. Ask him to go inside and get his shoes, and ten minutes later you see him completing a puzzle on the table in the hallway. On the other hand, there's little he misses. He reads the annoyed expression on your face and responds before you say a word; he knows his mother's approaching from the smell of her perfume and can identify most birds from their song.

b. Harris loves to get immersed in a puzzle or play with his cars and trucks. If he's engrossed in something, there is not much that distracts him. When his interest wanes, he'll leave his cars to see what cartoon his sister is watching or follow the smell of cookies baking in the kitchen. Most of the time he reads his sister or me well enough to know when to back off.

c. May is a whiz at taking care of business. She gets home from school, does her homework, then her chores, and can enjoy her TV program before bed. If you ask her to get something done, you can usually be assured that she'll do it, regardless of what's going on around her. Being so focused on a task to the exclusion of all else means she's not paying attention to the subtleties around her, such as a needy friend or a colorful sky.

Make it personal:

_____

_____

_____

8. Intensity: Refers to the child's depth of emotional reaction. What passion and energy does he bring?

Circle the letter that best describes your child's intensity.

a. It was great to hear my daughter's kindergarten teacher tell me, with loving appreciation, "I've never met a child who feels her feelings as strongly as Abigail." The intensity of her tears when we separated was only equal to her gleeful laughter when she played with a puppy, or her overwhelming frustration when she couldn't tie her shoe. She reacts passionately to most of life.

b. Maggie is a bubbly child. Her laugh is contagious. For the most part, she is even-tempered and without much drama, although you have to know her well to read some of her moods. When she's sad or afraid she will get quiet, but make her angry and she'll stomp off with great fanfare, loudly declaring she needs to be alone.

c. Richie is so smart and curious, even at eight years old. His sense of humor is intelligent and somewhat low key, and it's often hard to read his feelings because his reactions are so subtle. His friends appreciate his good ideas for games to play, and he's never competitive with them. For his last birthday, he said he really wanted a stapler for his gift—one of those little red ones with the small staples. When he opened his present, he smiled and said "Thanks!" and went off to do some stapling.

Make it personal:

_____

_____

_____

9. Sensitivity: Refers to the degree of awareness and reaction a child has to differences in sensory stimuli—*The Princess and the Pea* syndrome.

Circle the letter that best describes your child's sensitivity level.

a. Michael will only wear cotton shirts with an open neck, nothing too tight, and he changes his clothing at least twice a day. His diet is limited to meat and potatoes—more specifically, hamburgers, fried chicken, and french fries. The only green thing he'll consume is string beans. It drives him crazy if there's a hint of static on the radio or if the lights are too glaring, and he can smell things the dog barely notices. What a kid. With his sensitivity, he really can appreciate a beautiful piece of music and the smell of freshly cut grass much more than most of us.

b. Jane is aware of sights and sounds around her but can tune things out when she needs to. She loves visitors, so when she hears the dog bark downstairs she comes running to see who is at the door. If she's playing with her girlfriend, the phone can ring and ring but she ignores it. She likes soft blankets and appreciates the smell of clean towels, but won't fuss if she has to wear her wool jacket that's a bit scratchy. She can't sleep with the light on and she hates to have the sun in her eyes.

c. We were amazed when Ariel slept through the blasting of the cinder block wall on the back of our house. She could sleep through any-thing. As a first child, it was great that she didn't mind noise or lights or changes in her surroundings, since we often took her visiting family and friends on the weekends. These things just don't seem to faze her.

Make it personal:

_____

_____

_____

Note: All of the above examples came from real parents and their real children. *If you go to Appendix 1, page 231, you can read the specific strategies each parent used to accommodate their children's behavioral traits and challenges.*

Because temperament plays such an important role in behavior, we encourage you to use this assessment as a starting place. Become an expert in your child's temperament. Your parenting will get a whole lot easier and your understanding will help your child feel understood and seen.

> **TRY THIS:** *Just for fun, write a list of your child's most puzzling behaviors. Now look at the nine traits. Try to connect each behavior with any trait it relates to. Does a picture emerge?*

Acceptance

Remember Dr. Chess from Chapter 2, one of the pioneers in temperament research? After seeing her obituary in a New York paper, our friend Jim shared this story with us.

> *"When our daughter, Jodie, was six or seven my wife Lori and I took her to see Dr. Chess. We were concerned that Jodie was often moody and withdrawn and had difficulty with any new situation, especially if it involved new people. She showed little enthusiasm for the activities*

or adventures we initiated, leaving us with a feeling of inadequacy. We worried that her lack of enthusiasm and general negative presentation would affect her future friendships.

"After several sessions with Jodie, Dr. Chess met with us again and reassured us that Jodie was just fine—the problem was really about our expectations for her. For the first time we heard the term temperament. *She said that Jodie's inherited temperament made change difficult, especially when it involved new people or environments. Furthermore, she predicted that Jodie was not likely to become more noticeably enthusiastic or lighthearted, because it was her nature to be a bit gloomy, even a little grumpy. While empathizing with the challenge of having a child whose temperament was so different from our own, she encouraged us to focus on working with it rather than trying to change it.*

"While this was not easy for us to grasp or accept, we tried. It didn't happen overnight, but the less we worried and the more we accepted, the better things got for everyone. We found that humor helped and so did respecting her limits about new situations. Lo and behold, she had friends, and seemed perfectly happy once we stopped being unhappy for her."

Lori and Jim are hardly alone in their belief that their daughter would be happier if she were less moody and more socially adventurous. From a parenting perspective, it may seem logical that a more relaxed, or less sensitive, or more social, or better focused, etc. child would be happier. What we don't realize is that temperament is not something to be "fixed"; it's just a part of who we are. It is not only unrealistic to try to change a child's temperament, but it is also disrespectful.

Though it may feel counterintuitive, acceptance, not disapproval, is the best way to nudge or stretch a child's nature. Children feel confident and at ease with themselves when they feel understood and accepted. Most important, a child who feels good about herself is more open to and capable of stepping beyond what is currently comfortable.

Setting Limits

To avoid any misunderstandings, let's make the distinction between accepting a child's basic nature and letting her do whatever she wants. Acceptance means you respect the child as she is. It does not mean that all expressions of her temperament are acceptable. As her parent it is your responsibility to set limits, establish expectations, and offer guidance, teaching what is safe and appropriate. Temperament is not an excuse for bad behavior. Your limits and expectations should fit the temperament and ability of your child.

> *For example, your very active child needs outlets for her energy. Left on her own there is no telling where that energy might take her. No, it's not okay to swing from the chandelier or run over the dog with her shopping cart. Appropriate options are the rope swing outside or a race with the dog to the mailbox.*

> *Your young son, who is uncomfortable with new situations or people, comes in from play and ignores your visiting friend. Without a big fuss, you go to his room and explain that it is polite to say hello when someone is in the room. He does not need to stay, but he does need to come out and say hello to your friend.*

P.S. Children feel secure and cared for when they have limits and understand what your expectations are.

Helping a Child

When it feels as if your child is intentionally being impossible, it can be difficult to remember that his behavior is often a function of his temperament and not an intentional plot to embarrass you or drive you crazy.

Can you imagine the sense of confusion and hurt, even abandonment, a child might feel being punished or judged for behavior he does not understand and does not know how to control? It would be like expecting him to intuitively know how to drive a car or navigate a subway on his own.

We help our children understand and respect this complicated aspect of their personality by first understanding and respecting it ourselves. The more we learn and observe, the more our choices and reactions reflect that knowledge. We see our children wholly and embrace them with acceptance.

A young child needs you to understand and accommodate her temperament. As she grows older, it's your responsibility to take this understanding and teach your child about her temperament, its influences, and ways she can help herself deal with challenges that are specific to her. Sharing your knowledge and insights with compassion supports your child's self-acceptance and understanding. Recognizing and acknowledging when your child has managed a difficult situation helps ensure there will be more successes.

Acceptance and understanding of a child whose behavior makes parenting difficult may be a challenge at first, but your efforts to accommodate their temperament actually makes parenting easier.

At eight, Cory's highly persistent nature caused some to view her insistent behavior as annoying or unreasonable, even disrespectful. At a large family gathering a seemingly inconsequential belonging of Cory's, a sparkly plastic headband, got misplaced. Many perfectly good replacements were offered, but none proved acceptable. In fact, the more alternatives that were offered, the more agitated and insistent Cory became. Finally, all the adults threw up their hands in annoyance and frustration.

Cory's grandmother, although somewhat embarrassed, resisted pressures to discipline this "spoiled and unreasonable" behavior. Acting with an understanding of her granddaughter's temperament, she took Cory out of the fray and hugged her. She acknowledged how much Cory must care about her fancy headband and said she understood how difficult it was for Cory to accept this disappointment and "let go" of not finding it. Finally, after promising to help find it later, she calmly told Cory how she would like her to behave now. These actions, along with her grandmother's understanding, freed Cory from her previous intractable position and allowed her to do as her grandmother asked.

Accommodating vs. Indulging

Parents often express confusion between accommodating a child's nature and indulging the child. Here are some examples to help you draw a finer distinction between the two.

Rose is a low-persistence eleven-year-old. She has a demanding school project that is due at the end of the month. A bright child, she struggles to stick with things, particularly when they are challenging.

Accommodation: Dad and Rose break the project up into sections. They schedule meeting times to work on each section. Dad helps Rose keep to the schedule and sits down with her each day. When she starts to lose her focus, he may suggest a short break. When she gets stuck, Dad asks questions, offers suggestions, and provides the encouragement she needs to persevere. With Dad supporting her through each step, Rose completes the project on time while learning some helpful strategies.

Indulgence: Dad and Rose break the project into sections and schedule times for each one. Dad lets her know he is available to help. She struggles and isn't able to do it. The day it is due Rose has a meltdown. Dad lets her stay home from school and promises to write a note to her teacher requesting an extension for Rose to complete the project.

> *Philip is a very distractible six-year-old. He is excited to start an after-school club like his big brothers, who attend Boy Scouts and Little League.*

Accommodation: Philip very much wants to join the Cub Scouts. His parents decide that this could work for Philip if they take turns attending meetings with him. Each week one of them volunteers to help out, keeping one eye on Philip, helping him stay focused and not wander off.

Indulgence: Philip's dad goes with him the first day and explains to the leader that Philip receives special programming in school due to his distractibility. A month later, when the leader calls his dad to report that Philip is not ready to attend the meetings, his dad calls the higher ups to override the leader's decision and let Philip stay.

> *Rodney is fifteen and definitely a gloomy, glass-half-empty kind of kid. His maternal grandparents not only have a predilection for practical jokes, but they love cards and games accompanied by lots of good-natured banter and teasing.*

Accommodation: Rodney's grandparents are not going to change and Rodney is never going to be comfortable with their ideas of fun. When they come, he has permission to spend the weekend with friends, provided he spends one dinner or afternoon visiting and being politely involved. His mom also mentions to her parents that Rodney doesn't like practical jokes.

Indulgence: Rodney can leave whenever his grandparents come. If his behavior is sullen or rude when he is with them, his parents dismiss it without later discussing their expectations for more acceptable behavior.

> **TRY THIS:** *Think about a situation when it was easier to indulge your child than to accommodate him. Parents do this to assuage a child's difficult behavior in the short term, but find that their actions often don't serve him well in the long term. Was that true in your case? How did you feel about your decision? What alternative strategy would you try if you could do it over again?*

Assessing Your Child's Fit

The concept of "goodness of fit" comes from Thomas, Chess, and Birch. It refers to how well your child's temperament meshes with the demands and expectations of his or her social environment. Though it could describe the fit within a family or classroom, we use it here to talk about the temperament fit between you and your child. For example, it's a good fit when a mom's need to keep a regular schedule matches her child's strong need for regularity; or when a dad who tends to be socially adventurous has a child who is comfortable being in new situations with new people. In the extreme, temperaments and attitudes clash and we say the fit is not good. Think of an intensely dramatic child with an understated mother who thinks her child overreacts to everything; or the physically quiet musician/reader with a dad who lives for action sports and is disappointed that his child has no interest or aptitude for athletics.

Having said this, it might seem that a parent and child sharing similar temperaments ensures a good fit and easy parenting. This is often not the case. If you have a negative view about an aspect of your own temperament, you will probably have a negative view if your child exhibits similar behavior. See what we mean in these next examples.

> *What should have been an hour of homework often turned into two or three hours of anxiety and aggravation as Susan's daughter got distracted by noise, pets, thirst, the birds outside—you name it. For Susan it was like reliving her own stressful school years. She constantly teetered between feeling frustrated and concerned.*

> *Don had always been judged harshly by his father, for his too fussy, too sensitive tendencies. When his son appeared to have the same tendencies, Don struggled with his own prejudices and harsh judgments.*

Our personal experiences, our feelings about our own temperament, and our culture all influence the way we feel and react to behaviors associated with temperament. Once we identify these feelings and make a conscious effort to shift, expand, and even reconsider our attitudes, change and acceptance on our part become possible. Best of all, parenting gets easier and our children feel good about who they are. The following two exercises are designed to help you find that acceptance and new perspective.

EXERCISE: CHECKING THE FIT AND HOW IT FEELS.

A downloadable version of this exercise is at www.parentinginyourownvoice.com.

This exercise has two purposes. First, you see your temperament compared to your child's temperament. Then, you consider the attitudes you currently have about your child's temperament and label the ones that elicit strong positive or negative feelings. These are the ones that have the most potential to impact your relationship with your child and make it easier or more difficult to parent him.

In the chart below, fill in the spaces for parent and child with the temperament scores—(a), (b), or (c) from pages 27–31 in Chapter 2 and pages 96–106 in this chapter. (If you would like to add another child or a coparent's scores for later work, do so in the optional columns.)

TRAIT	PARENT	CHILD	OPTIONAL	OPTIONAL
ACTIVITY LEVEL				
REGULARITY				
INITIAL RESPONSE TO NEW SITUATIONS				
ADAPTABILITY				
PREDOMINANT MOOD				
PERSISTENCE				
PERCEPTIVENESS / DISTRACTIBILITY				
INTENSITY				
SENSITIVITY				

Now go back and star any of your child's temperament traits that elicit strong positive or negative attitudes on your part. You'll be using these in the next chart.

Before filling out the blank chart, below, we recommend that you completely read the instructions first. In case you're unsure or confused, we've included a sample chart below your blank one so you can see how Suzie's mother filled out hers.

Instructions: Using the blank chart below, write the starred traits from the previous chart in the column labeled "TRAIT"—one trait per row. Next to each trait, in the same box, include a brief description of how that trait manifests in your child. In the second column, labeled "REACTION," write whether you react positively or negatively to this trait. In the third column, write *why* this behavior causes a positive or negative reaction. (For now, leave the fourth column empty; we'll return to it later.)

To help you get started, we did a sample chart below your blank one.

TRAIT (And how it manifests in your child)	REACTION Positive or Negative	WHY?	

TRAIT (And how it manifests in your child)	REACTION Positive or Negative	WHY?	

SAMPLE CHART

TRAIT (And how it manifests in your child)	REACTION Positive or Negative	WHY?	
ADAPTABILITY— Suzie is easy-going.	Positive	We have three children and it is helpful to have one who doesn't argue with us or need things to be her way.	
ACTIVITY LEVEL— Suzie has a very low activity level.	Negative	For the most part, we are a family that enjoys outdoor activities like hiking and sports. Suzie doesn't get enough exercise and it is like pulling teeth to get her involved in activities the rest of the family likes.	
PREDOMINANT MOOD— Suzie is happy-go-lucky.	Positive and Negative	Suzie is so positive and upbeat, but I am not. This should feel positive, but all that enthusiasm and effort to "cheer me up" often annoys me, and then I feel guilty.	

With your feelings about your child's temperament identified and explained, you're ready for the reframing exercise. Reframing is the ability to see a behavior, situation, or attitude with fresh eyes, from a different vantage point. There is much wisdom to the saying that whether something is good or bad often depends upon your point of view. Think about the way you might describe the same trait of a friend as opposed to an arch nemesis. A friend's "confidence" might be a competitor's "arrogance"; "energetic or spirited" could get devalued to "difficult"; and a "persistent" pal might be seen as an "aggressive" foe. Nothing is inherently good or bad. Reframing the aspects of your child's nature that elicit strong feelings helps you see a bigger picture, have more appreciation for your individual natures, and open your heart. You judge less and find better ways to be helpful with accommodations.

EXERCISE: REFRAMING YOUR PERCEPTIONS.

The purpose of this exercise is to practice shifting, expanding, or altering your perceptions about your child's temperament.

Go back to the first trait from the chart on page 115. The idea is to consider anything that helps elicit a different reaction. So, if you now experience the trait as negative, consider how it might be advantageous to him or her in the future, in different environments, activities, and careers where this trait could be an asset. Inject some humor. Reflect on the history of your own strong feelings or reactions. If you felt positive about it, play devil's advocate and find a negative side. Ask yourself if the trait will serve her in the world as well as it's serving her in the family. Maybe it's a shared trait with you and it reinforces an attitude that he is "just like me," which of course he isn't. The idea is simply to become more neutral and accepting.

Give it a try. There is a blank fourth column on the right of the chart you filled out above. This is where you will write your reframed thoughts. Do this for all the traits you listed from that same chart. To give you a sense of how to proceed, we completed the last column for Suzie.

TRAIT (And how it manifests in your child)	REACTION Positive or Negative	WHY?	
ADAPTABILITY— Suzie is easy-going.	Positive	We have three children and it is helpful to have one who doesn't argue with us or need things to be her way.	Sometimes it's important to stand your ground and fight for what you want. Even a little disobedience might be a good thing. Always being the "good child" doesn't sit so well with her siblings. Maybe we should think about how to help Suzie be more self-assertive.
ACTIVITY LEVEL— Suzie has a very low activity level.	Negative	For the most part, we are a family that enjoys outdoor activities like hiking and sports. Suzie doesn't get enough exercise and it is like pulling teeth to get her involved in activities the rest of the family likes.	It's actually kind of nice to have someone in the family who enjoys different activities and brings different topics and viewpoints to family discussions. I notice I don't try often enough to encourage the family to do more of the activities Suzie likes, which would actually be good for her siblings. If I'm really concerned about exercise, I think she would love yoga.
PREDOMINANT MOOD— Suzie is happy-go-lucky.	Positive and Negative	Suzie is so positive and upbeat, but I am not. This should feel positive, but all that enthusiasm and effort to "cheer me up" often annoys me, and then I feel guilty.	I realize my guilt is less about Suzie and more about how I feel about myself. If Suzie understood that this is kind of the way I am and I'm okay, she would have less need to feel responsible for my feelings. I really do enjoy her enthusiasm most of the time and I could let her know in a funny way when I'm not in the mood to be all "smiley."

Reframing is a great life skill that can be used across relationships and situations. It encourages compassion, creative problem solving, objectivity, and expansive thinking. Knowing there are lots of ways to view the same situation or behavior frees us from stuck places: prejudices, our "buttons," or knee-jerk reactions. It gives us more control over our responses and freedom to choose our point of view.

TRY THIS: *Think about the last time you felt really annoyed, critical, or impatient with your child. What temperament trait ticked you off? Now reframe that trait in a positive light. How might you have responded differently?*

At the end of Part II you will be writing a Child Insight Statement similar to your Quality of Life Statement. In preparation for that, please answer the following question:

CHILD INSIGHT QUESTION #1:
What two or three things have you learned about your child's temperament? Write them here.

A downloadable template for Child Insight Question #1 is at www.parentinginyourownvoice.com.

There is much wisdom to the saying that whether something is good or bad often depends upon your point of view. Nothing is inherently good or bad. Reframing the aspects of your child's nature that make parenting him or her difficult offers you practice in shifting your perspective. This flexible way of thinking changes how you react to your child's behaviors. You can see the bigger picture, appreciate your individual natures and needs, and make accommodations with an open heart.

In Chapter 2, you identified, and perhaps even discovered, aspects of your nature that explain why you are the way you are. In this chapter, we took you through a process to identify *your child's nature* along those same nine traits. But we also asked you to step back and consider the impact her nature has on your parenting style and decisions. Now that you have the ability to see your child's perplexing behavior or natural tendencies in this context, you have a powerful new parenting tool.

CHAPTER 6 TAKE-AWAYS

- *Temperament explains important aspects of your child's behavior.*

- *You can work with a child's temperament, but not change it.*

- *Understanding temperament helps make expectations realistic.*

- *Your acceptance helps children stretch and grow.*

- *Unacceptable behavior does not make your child unacceptable.*

- *You help a young child by understanding his temperament and by making accommodations.*

- *You help a growing child by teaching him about his own temperament and giving support.*

- *Anyone involved in the child's life should know about his temperament.*

- *Recognizing how your temperament and your child's temperament fit brings helpful awareness.*

- *This fit can make parenting easy or difficult.*

- *No expression of a temperament trait is inherently positive or negative.*

My Notes and Questions

7

Your Child in the Context
of Development

Having looked at your child's temperament, rhythms, and intensity we turn to development to help us understand his behaviors more fully. Development explains and describes all the physical, mental, social, and emotional changes taking place in children throughout childhood. The study of development encompasses everything from their early skills of walking, talking, and using the toilet, to the later, more subtle ones of complex thinking and self-reflection. Developmental markers give us a reliable context in which to understand what's happening now, what's coming next, and how we can best foster his growth.

We are better parents when we can observe and think about our child's behaviors in the context of development. Our actions and reactions are then more appropriate and more supportive. Whether we are deciding how to best answer their complicated questions about death or sex, or setting limits on how much TV or computer time to allow, our knowledge of their developmental needs and abilities informs our choices. Learn about child development and you become the wise parent who knows what to expect at each stage, where to step in or step back, when to worry, and when to say, "It's just a phase," or "This is totally age appropriate."

There are many great books and online resources about developmental stages of babies, children, and teenagers. *We list some of our favorites in Appendix 4, page 267.* It is a complex topic that really does require a book, not a chapter. But we want to introduce parents to the main concepts of development so these ideas become part of your parenting toolkit. We can't overstate how profoundly it helps your parenting to be able to recognize that how your child is behaving or learning or moving or communicating may not be within her control. It may have a lot more to do with her age and stage of development.

Development as a Parenting Tool

We promise you that understanding about development will help you feel more confident and more in sync with your child. Here's how:

- **You understand the ebb and flow of his growth.** Behaviors that might otherwise be disturbing or perplexing have a context or explanation. Like knowing about his developing emotional or social maturity.

  One day you have a happy-go-lucky child and the next day it seems as though "no" is the only response he has. Though his negative and oppositional behavior is a challenge, you appreciate his newfound sense of self. This understanding tempers your reaction.

- **You're in step with her readiness.** Your expectations match her developing abilities. If your expectations are in line, your communications, reactions, and discipline are more likely to be in line. When parents' expectations are unrealistic, children feel inadequate, frustrated, or anxious.

  Observe any community sandbox and you will inevitably hear a parent scolding a child for her unwillingness to share. This might be a realistic expectation for a five-year-old, with her social maturation, to work on, but it is not for a two-year-old.

- **You know how to support his growth.** Your choices are guided by your child's developing abilities. Choices about play materials, learning opportunities, vacation plans, or decisions about safety are all better when developmental appropriateness is taken into account.

  You buy your two-year-old chunky crayons, not thin colored pencils, because his fine motor coordination has not fully developed. Your twelve-year-old is ready to stay home alone for an hour after school, but not her six-year-old brother.

- **You know how to explain things in ways that she can comprehend.** How and what you say to children, as well as how much, depends on their ability to understand. Thoughtful discourse also helps children manage unexpected situations and difficult feelings.

  When you cancel a long-anticipated trip to the zoo to help an ailing relative, your egocentric four-year-old is not likely to take the perspective of the sick family member. But if you acknowledge his keen disappointment and offer concrete plans to reschedule the trip, you will get better results than giving a lecture on the importance of helping others.

- **You know when he may need help.** If you know what to expect developmentally, you recognize when a child may be having trouble mastering a skill or moving through a process. Help is more effective in the early stages of any problem.

   As a kindergartner, Paul struggled with copying letters and numbers. He had equal difficulty with scissors and buttons. Concerned, his teacher suggested he see an occupational therapist who concurred there was a developmental delay in Paul's fine motor skills. He received occupational therapy and by midyear, he was on par with his classmates.

Finally, your understanding and timely support helps children feel understood and cared about.

TRY THIS: *Choose one behavior or skill you notice in your child that is presently changing and growing. Write what you see. In the next exercise, see if you spotted something the experts have written about.*

_____

_____

_____

_____

_____

_____

_____

_____

EXERCISE: CHILD DEVELOPMENT 101.

In this exercise you will see how development relates to behavior, growth, or learning.

Research your child's stage/age of development: for example, child development at age three. *(Check our bibliography of favorites on pages 271–273, or do a search online.)* Discover one new thing about your child's developmental stage—something children that age typically learn, or do, or practice. Perhaps it will be a skill they typically work on or a behavior they try out at this stage. Now, observe your child and focus on that particular accomplishment or behavior. How is she doing it "her way"?

Now that you have started your independent study of development, you probably realize just how big and complex this subject is. Don't worry; there is no need to take in twenty years of information when you have a one-year-old. Your education can slowly evolve, right along with your child's unfolding development. Your library of resource books and reference materials may also grow in time. We suggest you keep one or two favorite references close at hand.

> *When Sheila's daughters were young, she used her favorite child development book like a quick reference. If one of the girls behaved in a way that worried or confused her, she consulted the book and usually found some reassuring or useful information—like the time her four-year-old started having tantrums and getting sassy. The comparison of the "Ferocious Fours" with the teen years brought a smile of recognition along with a sigh of relief.*

Some Basics about Development

In our work with parents, we've found that there are some basic aspects of child development that are particularly reassuring and helpful. This is a beginning place. You decide from here what more you want to know to support your parenting.

- **Physical, emotional, cognitive, and social skills develop simultaneously.**

  *While playing peek-a-boo, baby Jason experiences the **emotional** pleasure of play and the give-and-take or flow of **social** interaction. He practices **motor** skills as he reaches and pulls the blanket from his father's face. **Cognitively**, he begins to understand the concept that something can disappear but still exist, and realizes that the words peek-a-boo **communicate** your desire for a particular kind of play.*

- **"Normal" is only a guide; children have different developmental timetables.** "Normal" includes a range of ages, with children rarely developing "by the book." It's more typical that your child will be ahead in one area, behind in another, and in between in a third skill.

  Although a majority of children will walk right around twelve months of age, walking at eight months or fifteen months is still within the "normal" range for that developmental skill.

- **Early development is not smarter or better, just earlier.**

  Four-year-old Donna began reading before she entered kindergarten. Bobby entered kindergarten with a love of books, the ability to read a few words, and an aptitude for retelling a story. By the middle of first grade, Bobby was the stronger reader.

- **Children grow in predictable sequences, but with individual variations.** Gender, temperament, environmental influences, and heredity can all play a role.

  Toilet training offers a good example of these possible variations. Most children begin to develop the physical maturation for control around twenty months, and are trained by age three or later. However, boys typically take longer than girls. A child with extreme sensitivities might be highly motivated for potty training because she cannot tolerate the feel of being wet or soiled. A child with two older siblings might be more motivated than an only child. Yet another child could have an inherited problem that makes control difficult.

- **Development may unfold in a predictable sequence, but it does not typically follow a straight line forward.** There is a natural ebb and flow, even regression, as new skills are learned and integrated.

  Sometimes growth in one line of development stops while energies are focused on another. Peter stopped saying new words while he focused on walking. Then he resumed talking.

  Sometimes there is regression or a step backward just before there is a significant developmental leap. One-year-old Sharon had been sleeping through the night for months. Unexpectedly, she became restless when put down for bed. She was often found in the middle of the night standing up in her crib. Soon after, Sharon took her first steps.

  Changes in the environment can create regression. Five-year-old Louie stopped sucking his thumb when he was three. With the start of kindergarten he returned to this earlier way of soothing himself. By Thanksgiving, with a renewed sense of comfort and safety, the thumb sucking stopped.

- **It is usually true that earlier developed skills form the basis for later developed skills.**

  Julie first learned to recite numbers in sequence. Then she used numbers to count objects, one at a time. Later she realized that this means you have a certain quantity of objects. Adding and taking away objects followed. And so on.

- **Though not always as overt as the early years, children's development continues through adolescence and into their twenties.**

  At fifteen, Ben's voice and body changes are as notable as his improved physical coordination. His abstract thinking is off the charts, but his reckless impulsive behavior demonstrates immaturity in another part of the brain. A possible explanation: The frontal cortex that houses executive function (it regulates impulses and gives decisions a second look) is not fully developed in the adolescent male until twenty-five or so.

- **Most brain function can develop or redevelop throughout life.**

  At two, Peggy broke her leg. When the cast was removed, she had lost the ability to walk. Within a few months of enthusiastic practice, she was back to where she left off.

EXERCISE: EXPERIENCING THROUGH HER EYES.

The purpose of this activity is to experience the world as your child might, given her particular age or stage of development.

Refer back to things you learned about your child's present stage of development when you completed the exercise Child Development 101, page 129. With this understanding, try to put yourself in your child's shoes, imagining how she experiences things, what she feels, how she reacts, and what new skill or understanding she is trying to master. How do you see the world around you? What can you do and not do? Is there a sense of frustration? Yearning? Power? What do you need or want from your parents?

Supporting and Enhancing Your Child's Development

The challenge of the twenty-first century is to integrate what we know about development into the structure of our culture. Presently, there appears to be a cultural tendency to try to rush the development of intellectual skills. Because of this emphasis on mental development, sometimes social, emotional, and creative development are overshadowed and get devalued. Righting this imbalance will take seeing children in a more holistic way, encouraging all aspects of development, and supporting each with opportunities for expression. What better place to begin than in the home?

As parents, we create our child's first and most long-lasting learning environment. This environment need not be filled with expensive singing and talking educational toys or exotic experiences. Simple everyday experiences, which connect us to our children and allow time for their natural process to unfold, nurture development best.

Here are our three favorite ways to support development in your child, at any age:

1. Develop a close responsive attachment with your child. Current brain research suggests that the best support for our child's developing brain is bonding with him and creating a language-rich environment.

We do this naturally with our babies when we sing, cuddle, comfort with our voice, respond to their needs, and smile into their eyes. As our children grow, similar types of experience—our focused attention, eye contact, hand holding, enthusiasm, and verbal communications—secure the bond.

Talking to children becomes increasingly important in their early months and years. Even before they understand our words or have the language to respond, our talk stimulates many kinds of brain development. When we narrate play and activities, describe what we see, label our children's actions, body parts, and feelings, read to them, and sing rhymes, we promote much more than language.

Bonding and language continue to be factors in development throughout childhood. Keep it simple and natural. Interactions such as bedtime rituals, dinner conversations, a project, talking over your day, a walk together, or just sharing a laugh all have the potential to enrich development. For older children, emails and texting are a way to maintain contact but cannot replace the impact face-to-face interactions have on development.

A special note to parents of adolescents: Just because your teenager has become sullen and uncommunicative, don't give up on talking to him. Remember, he is going through some intense developmental changes, and separating from you is one of them. Older kids need touch and talk (not just texting!), just like younger kids do. They need reassurance and support. They need to know that you are interested and involved in their life (even if they don't show it!). Give your teenager a hug. Ask his advice about something. Talk about a news event that's important to you. These are simple ways to keep the bond strong at a time when he's naturally (and appropriately) pulling away.

2. Value and encourage play. Play is the natural work of the developing child. From early on, the behaviors and actions of children are purposeful and directed. They explore, construct knowledge, expand imagination, make sense of the world, and practice mastery—all while "just playing."

The importance of play in development does not stop at the schoolhouse door. From the backyard to the playing fields, children continue to need play experiences that support growth. Their later "play"—theatre, clubs, sports, social gatherings, etc.—provide opportunities to practice skills, infer and test knowledge, grow their imagination, take risks, work on the give-and-take of relationships, recharge, work through feelings, and problem solve. Every area of development is enhanced when we create an environment that supports and encourages play, especially play that is open-ended and self-directed.

3. Understand and respect their process. Development unfolds in its own way, at its own pace, and differently in each child. Honoring our child's individual tempo and process of growth expresses our support and acceptance.

Remember that children have a natural push to learn and master new competencies. Trusting their process allows us to relax, step back, and observe as they practice new skills. If we inadvertently step in too soon with help, or react in a discouraging way, we interrupt their process. When we stop to watch, we see the skills our child is working on, and can then support her practice and the steps she's already taking.

Another excellent way to help children feel our respect and acceptance of their development is to avoid making comparisons with siblings or other children. Comparing has a way of diminishing individuality and inferring value judgments—like the belief that faster is better.

EXERCISE: ENHANCING GROWTH THROUGH PLAY.

The purpose of this exercise is to support your child's development through play.

Think about some aspect of your child's development you want to learn more about: physical coordination, cognitive understanding, speech, emotional skills, or social sophistication. Research how this typically unfolds and what it looks like at your child's age. Then, discover or create a play activity and/or provide play materials that will support your child in that area of her development. For example, a tricycle for motor skills; hide-and-seek for separation issues; a small harp for motor coordination and sound discrimination; singing for language development and imitation; lengths of fabric and a book about fairies or a curtain and some hand puppets for cooperative and imaginative play. More ideas: Read a story and make up different endings for problem solving; present a hot topic for debate and then switch viewpoints, taking the other's side to practice listening and reasoning skills; play chess for concentration and visual-spatial reasoning; play 21 Questions for deductive reasoning; make up songs, poems, or collage about a given topic for creative self-expression through language, music, pictures, etc.

Now, introduce that activity to your child, give her the basics she needs to get started, and then sit back and watch where she takes it.

Like temperament, child development is another useful lens through which parents can see their children, particularly when a child's behavior is perplexing to us. That's why it's so reassuring to talk to other parents with children the same age, to join parenting chatrooms, or to own a great child development book. Being able to understand the "why" behind your child's behavior ultimately makes you a wiser and better parent.

CHAPTER *7* TAKE-AWAYS

- Development describes the physical, mental, social, and emotional growth children experience from infancy to adulthood.

- Child development informs your parenting, steers you to more realistic expectations, and encourages compassion.

- Your knowledge of development helps you identify opportunities and create environments that nurture your child's development.

- Honoring your child's tempo and process of development communicates respect and acceptance and enables you to watch and support his natural push toward mastery.

- Delayed development, in any area, benefits from early intervention.

- All areas of developmental growth take place simultaneously, each representing an integral part of the whole child.

- Children do not develop by the book. Each child has his own timetable and pattern. The child who grows up more slowly still grows up.

- Faster is not necessarily better.

- Comparisons and acceptance don't mix. It doesn't mean anything that Sally walked sooner than Polly—except to the children being compared.

My Notes and Questions

8

A Fresh Look at Intelligence, Learning, and Creativity

In the chapters on nature and development, you opened your mind and heart to your child's individuality. When you understand and accept his temperament and developmental patterns, he feels seen and valued. Now we focus on your child's natural abilities. This chapter is dedicated to seeing and nourishing the individual ways your child is smart, learns, and expresses his creativity. The beliefs your child holds about these aspects of himself shape his future and deepest sense of personal value and purpose. As his parent and chief advocate, you play a key role in helping him formulate positive beliefs about his abilities.

Every child has gifts and potential waiting to be discovered. When parents and society help identify and appreciate these gifts, children feel smart and capable. Too often, however, our society and schools tend to focus on a narrow kind of achievement. Educators and parents who can expand their limiting views about intelligence, creativity, and learning will see the intelligence in all children, foster their creative potential, and teach so all can learn. They will help them find and fulfill their promise.

In this chapter, we introduce new research and new thinking that challenges traditional beliefs about:

- What it means to be smart.

- How people learn.

- Who is creative.

- How to measure success.

At chapter's end, parents often express relief, gratitude, and happiness that they have a new way to talk about, cheer on, and advocate for their child's unique gifts.

An Expanded View of Intelligence

Too often, if you ask a child, "What does it mean to be smart?" he will talk about "A's" on tests and being good at reading or math. And too often this view leaves no room for his particular talents and abilities to be recognized or appreciated. Children want and need to feel competent and capable and personally fulfilled. This can happen when they have a sense of accomplishment, experience the joy of success, and have the freedom to express themselves in their own unique way.

A healthy society encourages and values all the gifts of its children. We need the dancer and the physicist, the naturalist and the philosopher, the teacher and the entrepreneur. We can have this rich mosaic of talents and skills when people, starting as children, are helped to develop their gifts.

Psychologist and educator Howard Gardner was one of the first to question the narrow definition that intelligence is measured by the 3Rs, standardized tests, and classroom performance. He argued for an expanded view of intelligence that includes the many types of abilities that: (1) originate in the brain, (2) improve with time and practice, and (3) are useful and valuable to our society.

His theory of *multiple intelligences* further states:

- There are numerous intelligences that all mankind has to varying degrees.

- These intelligences work in concert with one another.

- Any intelligence can be improved, although there is a predisposition to how much.

---> THE EIGHT INTELLIGENCES [PLUS ONE]

Here are Gardner's seven primary intelligences with educator and psychologist Thomas Armstrong's descriptions. Later, he added an eighth, Naturalistic. Gardner considered, but never committed to, naming a ninth intelligence: Existential. (His lack of commitment may be partly explained by the difficulty of including it in an educational model.) We chose to include it here because many children manifest this intelligence, and it is easily misunderstood or squelched at an early age.

1. **Linguistic** or "word smart"

2. **Logical-mathematical** or "number/reasoning smart"

3. **Visual-spatial** or "picture smart"

4. **Bodily-kinesthetic** or "body smart"

5. **Musical** or "music smart"

6. **Interpersonal** or "people smart"

7. **Intrapersonal** or "self smart"

8. **Naturalistic** or "nature smart"

[9. **Existential** or "existence and universe smart"]

A detailed discussion of the individual intelligences can be found in Appendix 2, page 251.

As professionals who work with children and families, we feel Gardner's work has profound implications. When we embrace the logic of a wide range of intelligence, the rich, diverse potential of all children can be recognized and supported in our schools and homes. This view of intelligence provides a framework for knowing and understanding our children's gifts, and helping them feel pride in the ways they are smart. A child who knows his strengths and their value feels successful and optimistic. He is more motivated to tackle challenges and more confident to take creative risks or express different ideas.

Identifying Your Child's Intelligences

When we see our children from the perspective of multiple intelligences, we open the door to noticing and appreciating all their talents and abilities more fully. Here are several strategies to help you to see your child's intelligences. We'll save the most obvious one for last.

- **Provide varied opportunities for exploration.** Expose your child to a wide variety of experiences to find the activities she enjoys, skills that come naturally, and subjects she wants to know more about. Some ideas: take outings to the library, museums, art shows, storytelling events, performances, and other community activities. At home, provide puzzles, arts and crafts materials, music, physical play, sports, gymnastics, dancing, and word play. Technology, in limited amounts and with guidance, also offers opportunities for identifying areas of strength and interest.

At a baseball game Suzie showed little interest in the game, but was fascinated with the physics of pitching. It prompted us to buy the book, The Way Things Work. *It was a big hit.*

- **Ask people who know him what talents and interests they observe.** Typically, people see your child in different contexts and through individual lenses/perspectives and can offer helpful clues. Ask other adults who spend time with your child what they think his talents and interests are and why.

  Billy's parents would never have appreciated his affinity for the piano if a neighbor had not marveled at his amazing ear for music and mentioned Billy's frequent requests to play when he visited.

- **Consider family talents for clues.** Talents are often hereditary. Sharing information about relatives' gifts with your child, without pressure, may shed light on or awaken a child's potential.

  When Molly and her mom worked on a family tree, her mom added what was known about each ancestor's interests, talents, or work. A great-great-grandmother's love for painting inspired Molly to go through stacks of them in the attic, hang them in her room, and take a painting elective at school.

- **Finally and most important, observe her interests and activities.** Children, as well as adults, typically gravitate toward activities and materials that use their talents. Therefore, one of the simplest and easiest ways to identify your child's intelligences is to pay attention to the kinds of activities she naturally engages in without being prompted, and the subjects she likes to talk about that seem to spark her interest.

EXERCISE: LEARNING ABOUT YOUR CHILD'S INTELLIGENCES.

A downloadable version of this exercise and worksheet is at www.parentinginyourownvoice.com.

The purpose of this exercise is to focus on the independent choices your child makes in his daily life. His choices help you identify his natural strengths/intelligences.

List three things your child often does in his spare time, things he naturally goes to when no one directs him.

1. _____

_____

2. _____

_____

3. _____

_____

Now look at the list of intelligences, pages 143–144. Next to each of the activities above, write the intelligences that are involved. If there is more than one intelligence for any particular activity, include all. (For clarification, see examples, below.)

In the coming days, see if you notice other ways your child uses these intelligences in her daily life. Also note any other intelligence that becomes evident.

Below, parents describe three of their children's activities and connect them to possible intelligences.

> *Six-year-old Bo: (1) He most frequently plays with his Legos or Erector set. INTELLIGENCE: Spatial (2) While playing with his cars and trucks he builds houses, garages, ramps, and ladders. INTELLIGENCE: Spatial*

(3) When he's not building, he's on his bike or flipping around on the trampoline. INTELLIGENCE: Kinesthetic

Fifteen-year-old Jill: (1) She goes right to her cell phone and email messages after school. INTELLIGENCE: Interpersonal (2) She chooses time with people over watching shows or solitary activities. She puts everything down when there is a friend in need or a conflict to be resolved. INTELLIGENCE: Interpersonal (3) When alone, Jill writes songs with lyrics, expressing emotion with understanding beyond her years. INTELLIGENCES: Intrapersonal and Musical

Seventeen-year-old Jackie: (1) She has found several word game websites she goes to in her spare time. INTELLIGENCE: Linguistic (2) When she travels to other countries with school or family, she's the first one to learn phrases, calculate currency, and test her new skills. INTELLIGENCES: Linguistic and Logical-Mathematical (3) Although she can kick back with a TV show or movie, Jackie often finds new things to learn about. This year she started studying maps and memorizing the names and capitals of every country in the world. INTELLIGENCE: Visual-Spatial

CHILD INSIGHT QUESTION #2:

What two or three things have you learned about your child's intelligence? Write them here.

| |
| |
| |
| |
| |

A downloadable template for Child Insight Question #2 is at www.parentinginyourownvoice.com.

Supporting Your Child's Intelligence

Parents are in the best position to notice and honor a child's natural abilities. Here are the ways you can support their realization.

- **Consider your own attitudes.** We tend to support the activities and interests we think will be most important, useful, or acceptable for our children. Start by paying attention to your attitudes about your child's abilities and what you believe are worthwhile interests or activities. Be on the lookout for any biases you have that may lead you to overlook or undervalue your child's particular intelligence.

  Convinced that learning to play a musical instrument was the type of enrichment every child should have, Maxine overlooked her son, Isaiah's, propensity for crafts and working with his hands. She gave him music lessons, though he did not express any talents or interests in music.

- **Point out her competencies.** Make a conscious effort to let her know you appreciate and respect her abilities and natural gifts. Be specific, and give examples. Tell your child what you see as her strengths, and acknowledge when she uses them.

Raine was so adept at using the computer that the household relied on her help for any glitch that arose or instruction needed. Regularly, one member of the family or another said, "What would we do without you? You're not only good at the computer, but you seem to really understand how tech stuff works."

- **Provide opportunities to practice the things for which they show a propensity.** Offer your child time and materials, lessons and outings that allow him to exercise, explore, and develop his talents and abilities. Enlist his help with things at home that use his gifts.

  Steve loved to spend time watching birds. He was thrilled when we bought him a book filled with colorful bird pictures, facts, and names. When he was old enough to go on walks, he became one of the youngest members of the local chapter of the Audubon Society. That year, field binoculars were the perfect holiday gift.

- **Help others appreciate all the ways your child is intelligent.** Share your insights with teachers, relatives, and friends to help them recognize and support your child's strengths and weaknesses.

  April loved maps and charts and puzzles, but was not a terrific writer. Early on in the semester, her mom met with her teacher. They talked about ways to help April improve her writing. When mom explained April's talents and interests in maps and charts, they discussed ways to use her spatial skills to help with writing. Charting out the plot of a story first, before writing it, was one of the techniques that came out of this talk.

- **Leave room for growth and change.** Avoid too narrowly defining your child's abilities so that he fails to use other competencies or try things that come less naturally.

Though dancing did not come as easily to Jasmine as algebra, she took a class and loved it. Working harder on the dance floor than she was used to yielded enjoyment and pride in her accomplishments.

TRY THIS: *Think about your own strengths and interests growing up. Were there intelligences you had that got overlooked or went unsupported? Was there someone who helped you discover and strengthen an intelligence? Is there a long-forgotten intelligence you would like to nurture now?*

An Expanded View of Learning

Children are wired for learning. Motivated, curious, and driven to master new skills and challenges, they are sponges for information. No one needs to teach them how to learn. Children learn naturally when they take in and process information through their senses. We all learn this way, but there's one important difference: We do not all have the same mix of sensory strengths, also known as one's sensory profile. This means that learning, like intelligence, will be different for each of us. When learning the identical concept, one child with a strong visual sensory pathway might benefit from seeing a demonstration or picture, whereas another child whose touch sense is strong might learn by taking part in a demonstration or building a model.

Happily, children don't need to know their sensory profile in order to learn; they intuitively gravitate toward the sensory modality or modalities that are the most efficient learning pathways for them. This natural sensory selection process for learning can be thought of as her personal learning style—one that continues throughout life. With an expanded view of learning, parents and teachers recognize these basics:

- All children want to learn.

- Motivation is an essential component of learning.

- Previous success is a strong motivator.

- Our sensory strengths vary just as our intelligence strengths vary.

- Ideal teaching or instruction integrates all sensory processes and supports the strongest modalities of each child.

- The more sensory modalities you engage for learning, the more likely children are to integrate and retain what they learn.

- We empower a child when we help her discover her own learning preferences.

- When a child understands his preferred way to learn, he has a direction for choosing his own learning strategies and the knowledge to self-advocate.

Gregg's homework assignment was to read a chapter in American History and prepare for a quiz. He has two good strategies for reinforcing and remembering the material. To use his visual strength he makes a concept web, draws pictures, or constructs a timeline. To make use of his auditory strengths, he summarizes or tells a story out loud about what he read.

When Christina needs to learn her spelling words she starts by singing them: "C…A…T…cat!" The auditory input is reinforced when she makes use of her kinesthetic strength by writing each word a few times.

It was good teachers and informed parents who helped Gregg and Christina identify their individual sensory strengths and then use them for developing good study plans. When we help children be proactive and responsible for their own learning, they develop a sense of empowerment and a positive attitude about learning. Their success satisfies the natural desire to learn and encourages feelings of competence and confidence.

The Way You Learn

As with other discussions, learning is a big, ever-evolving, and fascinating topic. Our goal is modest. We want you to explore your own learning process so you can then pay attention to how your child learns. Recognizing that different children learn differently points you in the right direction. This next step gives you an introductory look at the three sensory modalities most commonly associated with the way we learn.

⋯→ THE THREE PRIMARY SENSORY LEARNING STYLES

1. **Visual:** The visual learner learns best with images and written words.

2. **Verbal:** The verbal learner learns best by listening or using language.

3. **Kinesthetic:** The kinesthetic learner processes information best through body movement.

Refer to Appendix 3, page 263, for more detailed descriptions of these learning styles.

SELF-ASSESSMENT: GETTING A FEEL FOR LEARNING.

The purpose of this exercise is to reflect on your own learning preferences by answering a few questions. It's likely that for some or all of the questions below, you'll have more than one answer. Circle them, and note if a pattern emerges.

1. If you wanted to remember a phone number, what would you do?

    a. Write it down and read it so you can picture it in your mind. (visual)

b. Say it out loud a number of times. (auditory)

c. Write it and push the buttons on the phone numerous times. (kinesthetic)

2. If you wanted to learn how to tack a sail, how would you do it?

a. Watch someone do it. (visual)

b. Listen to directions. (verbal)

c. Do it to experience the feel of it. (kinesthetic)

3. If you weren't sure how to spell a word, what strategy would you use?

a. Write it as you remember it looking, then see if it looks right. (visual)

b. Try to sound it out. (verbal)

c. Write it to see if it feels right. (kinesthetic)

4. If you had to assemble a toy, what directions would you prefer?

a. You'd like to watch a video or look at diagrams. (visual)

b. You'd like to read the directions out loud or have someone explain them to you. (verbal)

c. You'd like to try it. No directions—you'd figure it out as you went along. (kinesthetic)

5. When you want to learn and remember a song, which of these would you most likely do?

a. Read the words and visualize the images the words elicit. (visual)

b. Sing along while you read the words in text. (verbal)

c. Sing along and tap your foot or move your body to the music. (kinesthetic)

6. When you are learning a dance step, what helps you learn it best?

a. Watching someone demonstrate it as you practice. (visual)

b. Listening to someone explain the movements, talking you through them. (verbal)

>   c. Doing the movement once or twice so you remember it.
>   (kinesthetic)
>
> Did a strong preference for one or two learning modalities emerge? If you
> had a tendency to choose more than one answer, you're not alone. As men-
> tioned, effective learning often involves the use of multiple senses.

Identifying Your Child's Ways of Learning

Now that you have a feel for the different learning modalities, you're ready
to take a look at your child's learning preferences. Just remember: You're
an observing investigator, not an expert. You are gathering clues, following hunches, and putting two and two together. It may be that no defini-
tive picture emerges. Keep observing as the demands of school and life
change; you may notice learning strengths and weaknesses that weren't
evident before.

Here is a list of ideas to guide you in your quest to know more about the
way your child learns:

- **Ask yourself, "What is my child good at?"** Your child's intelligence
  offers clues to his learning preferences.

  *If your child is a good artist, he probably learns best visually. If she
  exhibits athletic excellence, she may learn best when her body is engaged in physical movement. (kinesthetic) The converse also applies.
  The child who cannot follow verbal instructions or discourse easily
  may experience similar difficulty processing verbal discussions in
  the classroom.*

- **Pay attention to what they do in their spare time (when you turn
  off the TV).** Children gravitate to activities that engage their sensory

strengths, providing you with insight into their learning preferences and direction for motivation.

Jamie loves to work with her hands doing crafts, knitting, and building models. (kinesthetic) Fred and Dennis are usually engaged in something physical like climbing on the jungle gym, or running around the play yard (kinesthetic), while Alice listens to stories and does word puzzles. (verbal) Dana likes activities like puzzles, blocks, mazes, checkers, or chess. (visual/spatial)

● **Observe your child's natural way of learning something new.** What study/learning strategies has he come up with on his own that work for him? What senses are involved in his learning?

Ricky talks himself through a problem and repeats information that he needs to remember out loud. (verbal) Sarah learns best while moving—pacing while she talks or writing out her spelling words over and over again. (kinesthetic) Ben creates visual pictures of what he wants to learn, and often understands better after making a visual web or map. (visual)

● **Reread old report cards or camp comments.** Old narratives by teachers and counselors who knew your child well may hold new meaning or relevance. Be alert to learning strategies that worked particularly well, areas of interest and strength, as well as areas of struggle or disinterest.

In first grade, Jackson's teacher realized that he remembered things best when he talked about them with another child. Interactive types of activities helped him to learn. (verbal)

CHILD INSIGHT QUESTION #3:

What two or three things have you learned about your child's learning preferences? Write them here.

| |
| |
| |
| |
| |
| |
| |
| |
| |
| |

A downloadable template for Child Insight Question #3 is at www.parentinginyourownvoice.com.

Supporting Your Child's Learning

Our goal as a parent is to nurture and sustain our child's natural desire and motivation to learn. When we see who she is, respect her learning process, and believe in her ability, we support a lifelong love of learning. These next ideas will help you on your way.

● **Success breeds more success.** Failure can be disheartening, and frequent failure can cause children to stop trying. We support our children when we find ways they can experience success.

Randy is ready and motivated to dress himself, but developmentally, unable to tie his shoes. Until he's ready, shoes with Velcro help him have the success of dressing himself. Mickey is struggling in chemistry. If he's willing and allowed to retake a test, he might be more successful after a second round of studying.

- **Consider your own attitudes.** Did those examples above feel like "cheating" to you? Prejudices about how we should learn or what constitutes real success abound—and they distract us from our stated goal of encouraging learning. They misdirect our focus on the degree of rigor, the speed, or the route that a child's learning takes rather than on her achieving mastery.

   Alice noticed she was always a little anxious when her son took longer to learn something than his brother had.

- **Make good matches.** Whenever possible, request teachers, create environments, and provide materials that complement, enhance, and support her learning preferences.

   Harry used plastic pie wedges to help him learn about fractions. Being able to see/visualize and manipulate the pieces helped him grasp the concepts and made use of his preference for visual and kinesthetic learning.

- **Fan the flame.** Observe and listen. When you see a spark of interest, fan the flame.

   At eleven, Curtis found an arrowhead in the neighbor's field. This prompted questions about who lived here before us. His dad took him to the museum and helped him choose library books about the indigenous people of their area. Curtis got hooked on local history.

- **Tell teachers what you know, and ask them what they see.** This give-and-take with teachers promotes understanding and provides support for both parent and teacher.

  Mark's teacher confirmed what his parents had guessed. She told them he had such a good auditory memory that he picked up much of his learning in the classroom lecture. It helped explain why his grades were so good despite little studying. The teacher followed up by challenging him a bit more on tests with essay questions that required analysis.

- **Encourage learning from a place of strength, not weakness.** On the heels of experiencing success, a child's confidence and motivation are high and she is in the best position to tackle more difficult learning challenges.

  Paula loved music and wanted to play the piano like her musician mother. Initially, playing by ear was much easier for her than learning to read the notes. Without any pressure from her mother, Paula continued to joyfully play by ear until she was motivated to tackle the more difficult task of learning to read the notes.

- **Teach your child about her learning style and help her develop useful learning strategies.** Discuss what you observe and ask what she's noticed. Help her to recognize and use these natural strengths, especially when material is challenging.

  After Kelly had a meltdown tackling a writing assignment, her dad reminded her that talking into a tape recorder first would help the flow and organization of her words.

- **Encourage all senses for learning.** Children naturally, and ideally, use more than one sensory pathway (visual, auditory/verbal, kinesthetic) to learn. While you encourage and emphasize their preferences, give attention to developing the senses that aren't as strong. The more tools they have, the deeper and more effectively they can learn.

  Caleb didn't have very good listening skills. To strengthen them, his mom played games that required him to pay attention to the details of the story she told. His improved ability to listen served him well in middle school and high school.

- **Get help when learning falters.** Any child can have trouble learning, even when instruction is ideal. Whether it is a developmental delay requiring professional assessment and intervention or a short-term difficulty with algebra, early intervention is best. Professionals can also help identify learning strengths and weaknesses and provide specific interventions and resources.

  After noting that Molly Rose had difficulty following multi-step directions and often seemed confused in class when complex concepts were explained, her mother consulted a learning specialist.

- **Involve yourself in the school community, even in a small way.** Your interest shows your child and her teachers that you care about her learning. Involvement in her educational community is a way to stay connected to this important aspect of her life.

  Even though she was an overworked attorney, Sarah's mom committed to attending one field trip a year so she got to know the teacher and Sarah's classmates.

An Expanded View of Creativity

Creativity is the inherent gift of every individual, and creative expression, the presentation of his or her unique self. In the face of cultural trends that attribute creativity largely to artists and inventors, there's little recognition that all individuals have the capacity for originality. An expanded view of creativity acknowledges that the ability to bring something original to the world exists within each person, because each of us thinks, experiences, and reacts in a way uniquely our own. No matter what form it takes, unfiltered creativity reflects the originality, imagination, vision, beauty, and resourcefulness in each one of us.

Young children openly express their ideas, artwork, songs, and inventions without filters or inhibitions. When your child's creative originality is consistently met with interest, acknowledgment, and appreciation, he learns that it is valid and worthy of expression. Your recognition helps him build a base of confidence and courage to put himself out into the world. A self-confident child is less vulnerable to the responses of others, and less likely to censor or repress his personal expression.

The child who learns, early on, the value of her creative gifts has a head start toward fulfilling her individual potential, heeding her voice, finding satisfaction with her life, and perhaps even becoming a force of change in the world. It's up to you to offer ample room for your child to fully express her originality. This section aims to help you create the kind of environment that allocates time, provides opportunities, and then applauds and encourages your child's creativity.

Identifying Your Child's Creativity

Besides the obvious products of your child's imagination, such as drawings, poems, and dance moves, many of her everyday actions and reactions are also expressions of her creative process. Look for them as you observe your child. Here are ways to discover your child's creative proclivities.

- **Notice how she presents things aesthetically.**

  Darcy had a knack for putting together interesting outfits, complete with quirky accessories that she found at the dollar store.

- **Observe how he approaches a problem and the solution he arrives at.**

  Johnny invented a way to pull the light on from his bed without having to walk across the dark room at night.

- **Watch how he tells a story or argues his case.**

  Dillon creates stories of another world filled with fanciful creatures and curious plots. David's dad marveled at his son's ability to negotiate his cousin's favorite toy away from him.

- **Observe the ways they use their imagination.**

  Tim displays remarkable originality in his practical jokes, while Aaron is a whiz at 21 Questions. Samantha has invented a chocolate chip cookie recipe.

- **Watch for it in all manner of original play, art, music, and writing.**

  You notice your daughter's daring attempts at symmetry in her block construction and her elaborate use of all the blocks.

A downloadable template for Child Insight Question #4 is at www.parentinginyourownvoice.com.

Supporting Your Child's Creativity

It's important to remember that creative expression takes courage and confidence. When you put your name on something you create, you are saying, "Here I am, for all to see." That kind of exposure is not easy. After all, your creation (a part of you) might be met with indifference, laughter, or even strong criticism.

Recalling the vulnerable nature of creativity, here are some ideas for encouraging your child's self-expression.

- **Make time for unstructured play, free time, and time alone.** Our tendency to fill children's lives with activities and play dates leaves little time for their own self-expression, exploration, or just moments to think or daydream. Create opportunities that compel your child to direct her own play, find her own remedies for boredom, and enjoy quiet time.

   Wendy felt so badly when her son didn't have an adult or child to play with that she often dropped everything to come up with fun projects they could do. One day, she had Saul play alone in the yard while she finished her work nearby. After a few moments of grumbling about being bored, Saul found a bucket and started collecting stones. Before long, he was building stone pathways and archways in the dirt for the ants and insects passing through, immersed in his creative pursuits.

- **Be circumspect with feedback.** Critiquing, correcting, and interfering squelch the creative process, especially in young children. As you become more aware of the ways your child expresses her original ideas and creations, you will get better at separating the timing of both appreciation and correction.

Evan's teenage room was filled with his funky collection of crazy postcards and outlandish posters. The mural of poems and drawings he painted on his wall was quite personal and moving. When he presented it to his parents, they saved the discussion about asking for permission to paint his walls for later on, and focused instead on acknowledging what he was sharing about himself in his work.

- **Bring imagination and spontaneity into your home.** Take advantage of opportunities to express and experiment with imaginative ideas and make-believe.

  Roy and Bette often made up stories, shared ideas for new inventions, and helped their children in the construction of elaborate fairy villages.

- **Model and support flexible thinking.** Creative thinking requires considering possibilities, trying them on, exploring outcomes. Be playful and encouraging and help your child feel safe enough to take mental risks.

  During car rides, Joy presented a situation like, the deer and chipmunks are eating our vegetable garden, what can we do? The children had to generate as many different possible solutions as they could.

- **Provide creative opportunities and experiences.** For inspiration and ideas, expose your child to a wide variety of creative experiences, including art, concerts, theatre, museums, inventions, books, etc. Offer a fertile environment with a variety of materials, opportunities, and open-ended time for her to experiment with her own forms of expression.

Nadia's family periodically heads to a thrift shop or junk store for an outing. Everyone gets a small amount of money to buy stuff to design an outfit, create a sculpture, or find a new use for something old. They put one night aside to share their creations.

- **Model the confidence and joy of creative expression.** When you can, maintain a playful, curious spirit and take a risk being original and inventive. Expressing your creativity in whatever form is right for you communicates the value and importance of using this wonderful gift.

  Normally Ben's dad is serious and all business. But his kids love when he steps out of character and creates the most imaginative and outrageous Halloween costumes and transforms their home into a house of terror.

- **Remember that all gifts are not created equal.** Every child may have the potential for creative expression, just by the nature of his individuality, but not every child easily finds its expression. Some children need an extra push of encouragement, or a bit more attention.

  Sandra often copies the drawings of her siblings or enters their play scenes rather than creating her own. With encouragement, she will venture a bit into uncharted territory by making up her own color design or doll house scenes. Her parents make a point of seeking her ideas or opinions first, thus pushing her toward more self-expression.

Before moving on to Part III, it's time to create Your Child Insight Statement based on everything you learned in Part II about your child.

EXERCISE: WRITING YOUR CHILD INSIGHT STATEMENT.

A downloadable template for Your Child Insight Statement is at www.parentinginyourownvoice.com.

The purpose of this exercise is to combine and integrate your responses to the four Child Insight Questions you wrote in Part II into one cohesive statement.

Don't be intimidated—this is not an essay test and you won't be graded for grammar, style, or organization! The idea is to come up with a single statement that really describes who your child is in terms of her temperament, learning style, intelligences, and creativity. There's no right way to do it. The only requirement is that it should speak to you and create a good picture of who your child is.

This process is similar to the one you used to create your Quality of Life Statement in Chapter 3. Start by rereading the answers you wrote for Child Insight Question #1 (page 120), #2 (page 147), #3 (page 156), and #4 (page 162). In the space provided below, combine them into a single statement.

To give you an example, here's what Annette wrote:

Erin's temperament style is one where she has lots of energy and is intense in her reactions. (We need to help her understand why others withdraw from her full-blown emotional reactions.) She's flexible in her need for food and sleep and has a cheery disposition. Erin's visual-spatial smarts make her fun to build things with, from snowmen to Legos. She seems very happy and learns best when she can use her whole body in the process. As a kinesthetic learner, movement seems to free her to think and problem solve. Hands-on learning experiences are great for her. Since she seems to be so good with thinking in pictures, perhaps using visual cues and images to help her study history or complex science concepts is worth trying. Building projects and working with clay as well as dance seem to be good mediums for her to express her creativity.

Now, write yours here.

My Child Insight Statement

_____

_____

_____

_____

_____

_____

_____

_____

_____

_____

_____

_____

_____

_____

_____

Each topic we covered in this chapter—multiple intelligences, learning styles, and creative expression—is worthy of its own book. But just taking a little time to expand your way of thinking about your child's individuality in each of these areas opens your mind to some important questions. *In what ways is your child brilliant? How does he take in and master his world? How does he express his originality?* As you continue to answer these questions, you will discover myriad ways to see and support your child's self-expression and self-actualization. The fact that you are seeing and supporting his gifts and abilities will help him appreciate his own bright mind and creative spirit.

CHAPTER *8* TAKE-AWAYS

- *Limited views about intelligence rob children and society of their valuable gifts.*

- *Children want to succeed. Our job is to help them with respectful support.*

- *Intelligence, learning style, and creative expression are hallmarks of our individuality.*

- *A child who sees his potential in a positive light feels hopeful, motivated, and capable.*

- *Motivation, optimism, and success promote learning.*

- *Learning happens when the body's senses take in information and process it.*

- *We typically use the sensory modalities for learning that come most naturally to us. Ideal instruction utilizes a multisensory approach so that all children have an equal chance to learn.*

- *Every child has the potential for creative expression.*

- *Fostering imagination and promoting self-expression support creativity.*

- *Resourcefulness, originality, imagination, vision, and beauty are all expressions of the creative mind.*

My Notes and Questions

Part 3

How I Will Parent

When we set out to develop the process in this workbook, our intention was to offer parents new ways to think about parenting. We also wanted children to feel seen and understood. We hope we've accomplished both. By the time you complete Part III and have your own parenting plan in hand, our hope is that you will feel less stress and more confidence as a parent.

You've arrived at the final part of the workbook where your creativity can flow and all you've learned in Part I and Part II come together. This is exciting! Let's look at the solid groundwork you've laid down in preparation for completing your parenting plan. You've discovered your unique voice, and practiced tuning in and listening to it. You've identified your temperament traits, those of your child, and the interesting ways those two sets of traits interrelate. You've defined your personal values, and have thought about what makes you feel happy and fulfilled as a person. You've also taken a thoughtful look at your child's qualities, including intelligences, gifts, learning styles, and developmental issues. And throughout Parts I and II, you've acquired a robust set of parenting tools, which we'll assemble and revisit in Part III so you will have your toolkit all in one place to use and refer to as often as you need it. This is quite an accomplishment! With all of this foundational work completed, you are ready to create your unique blueprint or plan for parenting.

In Chapter 9, you'll do a quick review of what you've learned about yourself and your child so far, and take an inventory of your parenting toolkit. In Chapter 10, we'll help you create your Parenting Priorities Statement, a vision of the person you'd like to see your child mature in to, and the life skills, values, and qualities you hope she will develop and embrace. Chapter 11 is your chance to creatively construct a cohesive parenting plan using your stated priorities from Chapter 10 and everything you reviewed in Chapter 9. In the last chapter, we hope to provide a reassuring perspective, inspiring stories, and then send you off with a light heart and a confident smile.

9

Revisiting What You Know— and Moving Ahead

I t is the knowledge and understanding we have acquired about our self and our child that forms the basis for a good relationship and keeps our parenting focused and personal to us. Parenting, however, involves more than building a relationship with our child. It is being conscious of the responsibility we have to our child to be the one in charge. As parents, it is our job to determine what's important for our child's future and to set the course that helps him get there.

This chapter has three purposes. First, it is a reminder and acknowledgment of how much you already know. Next, it is a review of Parts I and II, where you focused on learning about yourself, learning about your child, and developing skills and strategies for your parenting toolkit. You will want to have this knowledge fresh and integrated as you start this final step. Finally, we introduce the process that will become your model for creating a parenting plan that is personal and purposeful, as well as flexible and fluid.

Progress You Can See

Growth that comes gradually often goes unnoticed. Whether you realize it or not, your parenting is changing. Your increased understanding of yourself and your child naturally affects how you think and react as a parent. Perhaps you are more patient with yourself when you are uncomfortable in a new situation, or more appreciative of your son's ability to make people laugh. Remember, all growth counts, whether it's subtle shifts in awareness or attitude, or notable changes in how you act.

The following exercise is designed to help you recognize how much you've absorbed, perhaps without even realizing it, and how much you've grown in the course of doing this workbook. It's great doing this exercise, because parents are always surprised and delighted when they recognize that they really *have* progressed and changed.

EXERCISE: SEEING HOW FAR YOU'VE COME.

Fill in the blanks.

1. I notice that I have a different attitude about _____

_____

_____

2. I am more patient when_____

_____

3. I am more aware of _____ (self or other's) need for

_____

_____

4. I never noticed/knew _____ (self or other) could _____

_____

_____

5. I felt confident when I made the decision to _____

_____

_____

6. I stopped to listen to my child when _____

and s/he _____

_____

_____

7. I made time to _____

_____

_____

8. It is still hard to _____

_____

_____

9. I made my child happy when I _____

_____

10. It makes my child crazy when I _____

_____

_____

11. It is satisfying when _____

_____

_____

12. I _____

_____

_____

(Fill in the blank with an observation of your own.)

As you go forward, keep in mind that you are in the process of integrating new ideas and changing old habits. This doesn't happen overnight. Be patient with yourself when you forget or feel as if you could have done better. Just noticing is progress.

Reviewing Your Toolkit

Throughout Parts I and II we introduced concepts, skills, and strategies that every parenting toolkit should have. Here is an opportunity to see them all together and be reminded that you have a wealth of tools to use whenever you need parenting support.

My Parenting Toolkit

- **Awareness:** This is the ultimate tool. Every other tool is either helped by paying attention or dependent on our ability to be fully present.

- **Quiet Time:** We quiet the chatter of the mind so we can connect to ourselves and rejuvenate. To do this, we set aside time to be still and present.

- **Voice/Intuition:** We listen to our voice and intuition when we want personal guidance regarding what's best for us. To do this, we turn inward, still our minds, and connect to those gut feelings and that quiet "knowing" within each of us.

- **Journaling:** Whether you realize it or not, you've been using this tool throughout the book—in exercises and Try This activities, in the self-assessments and child assessments, and so on. Every time we journal—recording our observations, experiences, thoughts, or feelings—we can deepen our understanding, gain insight, or work through a problem. Journaling helps us clarify and reflect.

- **Acceptance:** We use acceptance to embrace the aspects of ourselves, our children, and our life that feel difficult and frustrating. To do this, we avoid judgments of good and bad; we attempt to clear away assumptions and biases so we can see what's really there.

- **Our Values:** We connect to our values so that we have touchstones to guide our actions and choices. To do this, we stay in touch with our ideals and principles—and consider the messages that our actions and choices send.

- **Proactivity:** We respond proactively in order to make thoughtful decisions and not react impulsively. To do this, we actively pause and use that moment of hesitation between an experience and our response to consider our best action.

- **Observation/Listening:** We use observation and listening to see and know someone more fully. To do this, we keep an open mind, stay present, and pay careful attention.

- **Knowledge of Temperament and Development:** We use our knowledge of temperament and development to make appropriate parenting decisions. To do this we educate ourselves and consciously apply what we learn.

- **Other Parents:** We connect with other parents for mutual support and to share resources, insights, and experiences. To do this, we seek out parents we feel comfortable with and trust.

- **Community Resources:** We use community resources for support and to expand the opportunities for ourselves and our families. To do this, we become familiar with what our community has to offer.

- **Professional Resources:** We go to professionals to seek information, support, expertise, or insight. To do this, we acknowledge when we need help, and network to find our best options.

EXERCISE: PUTTING YOUR TOOLKIT TO WORK.

A downloadable version of this exercise is at www.parentinginyourownvoice.com.

The purpose of this exercise is to practice using your toolkit from pages 176–177. The exercise is twofold. First we want you to think about those areas of your parenting that could use a little work or attention—the ones that would improve your confidence and enjoyment of parenting. Write these in column A.

Next, look back over your toolkit and think about which tools might be most helpful in each of these areas. Write these in Column B.

To illustrate, here are Marina's responses:

COLUMN A: Parenting situations I'd like to improve.	COLUMN B: Tools I can use.
1. I want to nag my daughter less.	Proactivity Other Parents (I'll ask my husband to give me a signal when I start.)
2. Sorting out whether my son's behavior is acceptable or not.	Values Knowledge of Temperament and Development Voice
3. Give my son and daughter more opportunities to develop their interests and cultivate their talents.	Observation Community Resources Professional Resources

Fill in your chart below.

This exercise is one simple way to set your intentions for growth, hold them in your awareness, and identify tools that will help you accomplish them. Whenever you come across a parenting situation that feels challenging, remember to come back and dig in to your toolkit.

COLUMN A: Parenting situations I'd like to improve.	COLUMN B: Tools I can use.

Looking Forward

In the coming chapters you will set your purpose and create a plan for parenting that works for you and your child, right now. Be aware, however, that the plan you develop is tailored to you and your child *at this moment in time*—not necessarily a year from now and probably not five years from now. As every parent knows, plans and parenting don't always go hand in hand. That's why we'll help you create a parenting blueprint that's flexible and adjustable. Children, by definition, are changing and growing, and life has a way of introducing the unexpected. While your purpose may remain constant, the way you execute it will certainly change as you and your child grow. Ultimately, it is the process you go through to create your plan that is important.

It might be helpful to think about creating and using your parenting plan the way a chef creates and uses an original recipe.

- First, he envisions a culinary goal.

- Because he knows about food and the chemistry of cooking, he then decides on the ingredients, proportions, and methods he thinks would work best for his dish.

- Once it is completed, he checks in to consider how he did. Did the chemistry work the way he thought it would? Did the ingredients and proportions work? Is there something that isn't right or would make it better? He makes his adjustments until he feels satisfied with the results.

- Finally, when he wants to change his recipe, because of dietary restrictions, unavailable ingredients, or just creative impulse, it is his knowledge and experience with the process that allows flexibility and good alternatives.

All your good work has brought you to this place. You know yourself and your child better, and you have grown as a parent in subtle, maybe even profound ways. Like the experienced chef, you have acquired a foundation of knowledge and understanding that allows you to venture into the next creative phase of parenting—problem solving and blending together all you have learned into a personal plan. Your insights, awareness, and good tools are sharpened and fresh in your mind. You are ready for the next task, where you will take charge and state the intentions that will direct your parenting.

CHAPTER *9* TAKE-AWAYS

- *You have grown as a parent in concrete and notable ways. When you acknowledge this growth, it motivates and encourages you to keep growing.*

- *Your parenting toolkit is full of resources, ideas, strategies, and personal wisdom. Keep your toolkit handy and your tools honed with frequent use and practice.*

- *When you want to focus on a personal or parenting change, pick the tools that best support that growth.*

- *Parenting needs to flow and shift with changes in you, your child, and your circumstances.*

- *As you think about creating your parenting plan, consider the chef who learns to blend and highlight individual ingredients with his own personal instincts and creative touches.*

My Notes and Questions

10

Naming Your Parenting Priorities

P arenting priorities are personal commitments you make, based on a
vision you have for your child. They reflect what you think is important for your child's happiness and well-being, both now and in the
future. Parenting priorities focus on the qualities, skills, or behaviors you
want to encourage and the experiences you want to emphasize. They direct
you as a parent.

We name our parenting priorities for the same reasons we named our
values. The process brings our priorities to the forefront and into our
consciousness. When we are reminded of and guided by what's important, we feel confident in our choices and more relaxed about things of
lesser concern. (We might come to see, perhaps, that his hair color or her

gaudy taste in clothes is not so important after all.) With a clear vision of what we are ultimately trying to achieve, we know what to do and why we are doing it. As a result, we become more consistent and confident in our parenting decisions.

Parenting with the "End in Mind"

The "end in mind" is another expression we borrowed from Steven Covey's *The 7 Habits of Highly Effective People.* He says that any endeavor we undertake needs to have purpose and direction. We need to know where we are going before we can create the plan for getting there.

It was like that for the chef and it is like that with parenting. When you know what you want to achieve, you can create the steps and plan for how to get there. Naming your priorities sets the direction and purpose for your parenting. It provides a basis for decision making and the criteria to assess how you are doing as you go along.

TRY THIS: *Reflect on a recent decision you made as a parent. How did you make that decision? What was your process? Was it an off-the-cuff decision? Did you take time to consider it? Did you feel clear? Confused? Confident? Now that you think about it, would you change your decision? How did your process work for you?*

EXERCISE: IDENTIFYING YOUR PARENTING PRIORITIES.

A downloadable version of this exercise is at www.parentinginyourownvoice.com.

At the end of this three-step exercise, you will have your very own parenting mission statement.

Step 1: Ready, Set, Dream

The aim of this first step of the exercise is to brainstorm the raw material and ideas and then create a master list of intentions or priorities.

Get in a quiet frame of mind. Close your eyes, if helpful. Imagine your daughter or son as an adult, ready to go out into the world. Now imagine giving her or him the most useful, valuable, nonmaterial gifts for a successful journey. What are your deepest wishes for him? What does she need to know? What qualities will serve him best? What's important? What will sustain her? Don't filter or edit your responses. Just let your thoughts bubble up and out.

Now bring yourself back to the present and write down those thoughts. When doing this, it's not unusual to think of things that you either appreciate in yourself or wish you had more of. Go with these, if they came into your mind; they are valid. If helpful, consult the examples below before you do any writing.

Here's what Adi's parents, Dave and Beth, each wrote:

> *Dave—I'd like Adi to know how to:*
>
>> *- Deal with money.*
>>
>> *- Deal with work/employment.*
>>
>> *- Have positive relationships.*
>>
>> *- Care for her health.*

Beth—What I want for Adi:

> *Confident…think for herself…use her gifts well…a good educa-*
> *tion…exposure to many cultures…self-reliant…good manners…*
> *know about nature, the arts, and events outside her world…speak*
> *well…a good work ethic…manage money well…critical think-*
> *er…know how to cook…respect others… see the best in people.*

Notice the different ways Dave and Beth responded. There's no right way.

Write your initial thoughts here: _____

_____

_____

_____

_____

_____

_____

_____

_____

_____

_____

_____

_____

_____

_____

_____

_____

Now, leave this list and plan to return to it later. Once you have some distance and a fresh mind, revisit your list, and reconsider and refine what you
wrote above. Omit any ideas that no longer feel important, and add new
ones that make the list feel complete and most relevant. These are your
parenting priorities.

Step 2: Categorize and Define Your Priorities

The purpose of Step 2 is to organize your priorities into categories and reflect on what each means to you.

Using your list from Step 1, organize your priorities into five general categories on the lines below (page 190). If helpful, have a look at how Dave and Beth did their lists before you proceed.

Dave found that his list was already in general categories, but that he needed to add a fifth. After some thought, he came up with "Fulfillment/meaning."

Out of her list from Step 1, Beth came up with these five categories: self-awareness and confidence, self-sufficiency, self-care, relationships, and spiritual beliefs/world view.

Next, take each category and give a detailed description (skills, accomplishments, responsibilities, insights, understandings, knowledge, etc.) that illustrates its most important elements.

For example, Dave's category, Positive Relationships, included: "Adi knows how to communicate and listen; can empathize with others, is clear in her individual voice, and respects that of others."

Here are Beth's five categories of priorities and descriptions:

*1 – **Self-awareness and confidence:** Adi knows herself and trusts her voice, knows how she learns, and understands her strengths/talents and interests.*

*2 – **Self sufficiency:** Adi is independent and capable of meeting her work commitments, budgets her money efficiently, cares for and*

maintains her belongings, and is capable of daily living skills like
cooking, cleaning, etc.

*3 – **Self-care:** Adi knows how to care for her health, hygiene, and*
safety, knows the qualities of a trusted friend, chooses healthy situa-
tions and relationships, and asks for help when she needs it.

*4 – **Relationships:** Adi has communication skills, people skills, and a*
sense of community, responsibility, and charity.

*5 – **Spiritual beliefs/world view:** Adi has clear ethics to live by, a re-*
lationship to the natural world, meditation practice and/or traditions
that connect her to family and community, and appreciates the value
of learning and experiencing things outside her world.

Now it's your turn. In the spaces below, list your five categories of priorities, from page 188, and describe specifically what each means to you.

1. _____

_____

_____

2. _____

_____

_____

3. _____

_____

_____

4. _____

_____

_____

5. _____

_____

_____

Step 3: Create My Parenting Priorities Statement

As you did with your values in Chapter 3, this final step involves creating a statement of intention that includes the five priorities you listed above. Think of it as your mission statement for parenting.

Here is Dave's Parenting Priorities Statement:

It is my intention to raise Adi to be a confident young woman who is capable of working hard like her dad, feeling fulfilled in a job she loves. Of course, I hope she can also make enough money to live her life independently (needing only occasional support from us, and hopefully even supporting us in our old age!). I'd like her to have rich, satisfying relationships and be someone I like spending time with. I'd like her to be healthy and fit so she outlives me, because I couldn't stand to lose her.

Your Parenting Priorities Statement is a reminder of what you believe is most important for your child's future. As with your Quality of Life Statement from Chapter 3, use whatever form works best for you. Think it through and write it in a way that enlivens your commitment with enthusiasm, joy, and conviction.

My Parenting Priorities Statement

_____

_____

_____

_____

_____

_____

_____

_____

_____

_____

_____

_____

_____

_____

_____

_____

_____

_____

_____

The added benefits of establishing your priorities for parenting are:

- You have a clear vocabulary for sharing these ideas with others.

- You can check in from time to time to make sure that you are actively supporting your child's growth in these directions.

- You have a reference you can reflect on and revise as change and growth occur.

Two Parents, Two Lists

As with Dave and Beth, you may find your priorities are actually very similar. This occurs more times than not. It's also possible that your lists of parenting priorities look quite different. Here's where your ability to step back and really listen to each other pays big dividends. Understanding and respecting one another's priorities is an extension of respect for him or her as an individual. It builds good relationships and helps both of you be better parents. When parents honor each other's priorities, children receive clear and consistent messages and take comfort in knowing what to expect.

Having trouble accepting your coparent's priorities for your child? Return to Chapter 1, page 18, for guidelines on discussing differences, handling conflict, and balancing your two voices.

We know that you cannot plan the course of your child's life, nor can you predict what kind of person he or she will become. Life is full of surprises, and children are individuals who have their *own* priorities, goals, and desires. Nevertheless, when we as parents take the time to define our priorities, we create a vision or an intention for parenting. The Parenting Priorities Statement you wrote in this chapter will serve as a helpful beacon to gently guide you when you waver along your parenting journey and need some direction.

CHAPTER *10* TAKE-AWAYS

- *Parenting priorities reflect what you think is important for your child's happiness and well-being, both now and in the future.*

- *Priorities set the direction and purpose for your parenting.*

- *Decisions large and small are clearer when based on your priorities.*

- *Naming your priorities provides language for communicating your goals with others.*

- *Coparents who can communicate and respect one another's priorities are best able to provide clear, consistent messages to their children.*

- *Priorities may need to be revised as individuals grow and circumstances change.*

My Notes and Questions

_____

_____

_____

_____

_____

_____

_____

_____

_____

_____

_____

_____

_____

_____

_____

_____

_____

_____

_____

_____

_____

_____

_____

_____

Putting Your Plan Together

Congratulations! You have arrived at the penultimate chapter of this workbook, where you will assemble all that you have learned about yourself and your child into a working parenting plan. Having completed the chapters and exercises in this book, you now have new ways of understanding your child, creative problem-solving tools, and a strong sense of yourself and your parenting priorities—the basic elements for parenting your child, your way.

This is the moment when you go back through your work and put it all together, a lot like our experienced chef did when he assembled all his carefully considered ingredients into a satisfying dish. In this case, your Quality of Life Statement (page 53), your Child Insight Statement (page 167), and your Parenting Priorities Statement (page 192) provide the core ingredients. When blended together, they become your own proprietary recipe for parenting that's tailored to you and your child. Your recipe will need to be tested, tweaked, and adjusted, but the basic ingredients and process are there to guide you as life and children change.

Your Three Guiding Statements

Throughout the workbook, you created three important statements that capture essential aspects of you, your child, and your role as a parent. Each statement integrates new insights with what you deeply believe and intuitively "know." Together, they represent the foundation for your parenting decisions and serve as your best reminder of what's important for you and your family. Revisiting and recording those statements now will prepare you for the next exercise. If you feel moved to revise one of your statements, that's great, because you want each to reflect all you have learned and know now.

1. **My Quality of Life Statement**—connects me with my values and directs every part of my life. When I align my values with my voice, and my actions with my values, my life has integrity.

Write yours from page 53 here:

_____

_____

_____

_____

_____

_____

2. **My Child Insight Statement**—reminds me of my child's essence and the important ways he is an individual in his own right. It directs the quality of my relationship with my child. When I see him as an individual, it strengthens his emerging voice and self-esteem.

Write yours from page 167 here:

_____

_____

_____

_____

_____

_____

3. **My Parenting Priorities Statement**—connects me with my intentions for parenting, and those skills, attitudes, experiences, and abilities I feel are essential for my child's future well-being. It directs my parenting. When I align my actions with my priorities, I parent clearly and consistently.

Write yours from page 192 here:

_____

_____

_____

_____

_____

_____

Many parents tell us that just seeing these three statements together feels very powerful and grounding. They also represent a great deal of thought and work on your part.

Your Parenting Plan

With renewed insight and purpose, it's time to create your personal blueprint for parenting. You begin with the detailed list of priorities you created on page 192. While holding your child's individual needs in mind, you will add specific actions, activities, and resources that support those priorities. Like the chef, you can use and reuse this process, altering the actions and activities, finding new resources, and addressing changing needs as they arise.

EXERCISE: CREATING YOUR CUSTOMIZED PARENTING PLAN.

The purpose of this exercise is to practice translating your parenting intentions into concrete actions.

Column A: Go back to the five parenting priorities you listed in Chapter 10, pages 190–191. Write one parenting priority in each box of Column A, followed by your detailed descriptions for that priority.

Column B: First, reread My Child Insight Statement, page 199. Next, for each priority, answer the following question:

What actions or activities will foster this priority, taking into consideration my child's age, strengths, intelligences, interests, needs, learning styles, etc.?

Don't be concerned right now with details and practicalities. For now, just dream big and let your creative mind flow. Don't worry about *how* you're going to turn your intentions into reality. There will be time for that later.

Write your ideas in Column B, next to the corresponding priorities. (Leave Column C blank for the moment.)

Note: We included an excerpt of Beth's parenting plan for six-year-old Adi below the blank chart for you to refer to as an example. Her five priority statements are in Chapter 10, pages 189–190, if you want to refer to them for clarification.

My Parenting Plan

A downloadable template for My Parenting Plan is at www.parentinginyourownvoice.com.

A. Priorities	B. Actions	C. Resources
(1)		

A. Priorities	B. Actions	C. Resources
(2)		
(3)		

A. Priorities	B. Actions	C. Resources
(4)		
(5)		

An Excerpt of Beth's Parenting Plan for Adi

A. Priorities	B. Actions	C. Resources
Relationships: communication skills, people skills, a sense of community, responsibility and charity.	1. Organize a small play group. 2. Find suitable community events for her to participate in. 3. Volunteer with her at a Toys for Tots program.	1. Dave works with two people with same age kids. Invite them. 2. Community garden, library fair. 3. Toys for Tots website.
Self-awareness and confidence: knows herself and trusts her voice, knows how she learns, understands her strengths/ talents and interests.	1. Find opportunities and places for ice-skating and ice-skating lessons. 2. Help her connect to her voice by asking about her feelings. Model by describing my own feelings. 3. During dinner, ask for her opinion. 4. Have her create this year's family holiday card.	1. Aunt has a skating pond nearby. Older cousin Adi likes skates well. Will ask her to give lessons. 2. Reread Chapter 5. 3. Come up with topics— from articles, politics, movies, youth culture, etc.—that make for Adi-focused conversation. 4. Arts & crafts materials.

A. Priorities	B. Actions	C. Resources
Self-sufficiency: independent and capable of meeting her work commitments, budgets her money efficiently, cares for and maintains her belongings, capable of daily living skills like cooking, cleaning, etc.	1. Help her save for the snowcone machine she wants. 2. Adi helps prepare one meal a week. She can choose recipes. 3. Start planning and building a teepee.	1. Allowance. 2. Patient Grandpa babysits on Sundays and loves to teach her to cook. 3. Will take her to library for research and find someone to help actually construct one. I'll trade computer help with this person.

Column C: With these resources fresh in your mind from the Try This activity above, go back to your Parenting Plan chart. For every action in Column B, list resources to support it in Column C. (Refer to Adi's Column C, for examples.)

WELL DONE!

You now have practice creating a working plan for parenting—one that honors what you think is important and who your child is right now. Refer to it, play with it, and revise it. For it to be most useful, keep it alive and relevant.

Reflecting on Your Plan

Making a plan provides guidelines and promotes action. Executing the plan gives you feedback and a way to keep track of how you're doing. What worked or didn't work? Were you able to ask for help and find good resources? Have you misunderstood something? Where did you get side-tracked, and what actions offered you the best outcome?

As the developmental psychologist Howard Gardner puts it:

> "…unless one has the opportunity to think about what one is do-ing and to reflect on what went well, what went poorly, and why, the chances for a long-term improvement curve are slight. Time for individual and joint reflection must be built in…"

You want your plan to be fluid and flexible so that revisions and updates happen as needed. Stay tuned to your experience while executing your plan. If an activity loses energy or appropriateness or usefulness, it's time for a change. As you practice parenting with awareness and intention and feel more confident in your knowledge of yourself and your child, revisions will come more naturally, like the experienced chef who no longer needs to rely on a recipe but trusts his knowledge of the ingredients and how they work best together.

Naturally, there will be times when your parenting plan is not in the fore-ground of your awareness. Maybe your priorities have even slipped from memory. Here's a trick for those times of overload or confusion: Go backwards. If you are about to make a decision but feel ungrounded or unsure, ask yourself, *"Why am I making this decision or choice? What am I promoting?"* Your answer may trigger one of your stated priorities. That's great. If you realize the answer goes against a value or an intention, you now have an opportunity to reconsider your choice.

Practice helps. Think about your values, your child, and your parenting priorities as you develop ideas for the three real-life situations in this next practice exercise. Its purpose is to give you practice planning, making decisions, and taking actions that are based on what you know and what matters to you.

EXERCISE: PUTTING IT ALL TOGETHER.

Respond to each situation as if it were occurring now to your family, with your child at his or her present age. Be as creative as possible with your ideas and resources, but be true to who you are, who your child is, and your parenting vision.

And by all means, keep your three statements (pages 198–199) and tools list (pages 176–177) handy.

Situation #1: There is not enough time in the day to do everything that needs getting done. You frequently feel frustrated, alone, and/or exhausted. What do you change, introduce, and/or delegate to create a more balanced family picture?

_____

_____

_____

_____

_____

_____

Situation #2: Your child is about to start something new. It could be an unfamiliar babysitter, change of school, or a new job. How does she react? How do you best prepare her?

_____

_____

_____

_____

_____

Situation #3: Think of a familiar scenario that occurs in your household that you dread. It could be sibling conflict, negotiating weekend activities, even something like bath time. Now, create a new way to approach this scenario or to handle the dreaded aspect of it using what you've learned. Refer to tools and resources as well as to your statements and plan. Write it here.

_____

_____

_____

_____

_____

Dealing with the "Workshop Phenomenon"

It happens often. We attend an exciting workshop where we learn a new skill or a new way of thinking, and then return home filled with enthusiasm and ideas. We remember and try things out for a few weeks, only to gradually revert to our old familiar way of doing or thinking. Those who study the dynamics of change find that it takes three months of consistent practice to make a new behavior "stick."

As much as we would love to believe everyone will complete this workbook and then parent consistently using all their new tools and insights, we know this is not realistic. The best way to avoid the gradual slide into the old and familiar is with planned activities and support that act as reminders and reinforcement. That's why we strongly suggest you follow the 3R steps, below, which buttress the changes you've made and help internalize these new ways of thinking and responding. This follow-through helps assure your continued understanding, growth, and confidence as a parent.

FIRST: Reflect

Reflection is the most useful way to create positive changes in your life. Make time regularly to think about your parenting experiences. Now that you know where you want to go, take the time to ask yourself, "How's it going?" Journaling is a way to talk to yourself. Whether or not you have been sharing the process of this workbook with others, journaling is a useful reflection tool. Take time daily, or at least weekly, to sit down and reflect on your parenting. Check inside and see how grounded you feel in your parenting. Are you connected to your values and voice? Are you connected to your child? Does he feel seen? Are you able to keep your priorities in mind? Are you acknowledging your mistakes or shortcomings without judgment? Is there a place where acceptance is difficult? Try keeping a parenting journal for three months.

If you have been doing this workbook in a group, with a partner, or coparent, commit to continuing to meet for three more months. Together, talk about parenting challenges that have come up. Identify self-critical chatter. Reflect on ways to handle these challenges, reminding one another of useful tools and insights. Keep your dialogue going and your plan alive.

SECOND: Revisit

Read over your plan, your list of tools, and your three statements regularly for the next three months. Actively consider them when you are unsure of how best to respond or what parenting choice to make. Revise your statements as needed. Return to the book for reminders and to refuel your enthusiasm or to reconnect with your tools.

THIRD: Reinforce

Continue to acknowledge the changes you notice in your parenting. Write about them or tell others. Celebrate any shifts in thinking, reacting, or new ways of seeing your child. By *acknowledge* or *celebrate,* we mean pay attention to your growth. Be wary of the self-critical chatter that stands between you and feeling good about what you've accomplished. When you notice and acknowledge your new skills or different perspectives, it strengthens and reinforces them, just as it does for children. Take it a step further. Ask yourself how you can continue to use this new tool or insight.

By practicing the three R's—reflect, revisit, and reinforce—for three months, you integrate all the knowledge, insights, and tools you've gained so they come naturally and will automatically guide your parenting choices and actions.

The art of parenting is about knowing what's right for you and your family, and then working toward that end. The Parenting Plan you created and the work of these eleven chapters provide a solid foundation and template for your parenting. When "how to" questions come up, you have the wisdom of your voice, knowledge about your child, and many good resources to guide you to your best options. *Everything you need, you have.* So relax and trust yourself as we share a few last thoughts about being a "good enough" parent and enjoying the journey.

CHAPTER *11* TAKE-AWAYS

■ *Your three statements are reminders of the core ingredients for your parenting recipe or plan. Update them as needed. Refer to them regularly.*

■ *When your actions follow your priorities, you parent with clarity and consistency.*

■ *To stay on track with your parenting priorities and intentions, remember to regularly ask yourself, "Why am I doing this?"*

■ *A fluid and flexible parenting plan can be adapted as children grow and circumstances change.*

■ *If you reflect on, revisit, and reinforce all you've learned for at least three months, you are more likely to integrate and maintain new insights and growth.*

My Notes and Questions

Keeping Lightness and Enjoyment in Parenting

For eleven chapters you have "worked" to grow your understanding, consciousness, acceptance, and intention for parenting. Everything you need, you have, or know where to find to feel self-assured and relaxed. *Self-assured? Relaxed?* Maybe those aren't the words that instantly come to mind when you think about your parenting.

Consider this father's reluctant and disheartened confession at one of our workshops:

> *"I hear other parents talk about the joys of parenting, but mostly I feel an overwhelming sense of responsibility and inadequacy."*

Bravo, Jackson, for having the courage to say out loud what many parents feel at one time or another! There is no denying the work and responsibility of parenting, but that is not where we want to leave you. This final chapter is dedicated to Jackson and every other parent who has ever felt that they were not good enough, or struggled feeling more responsibility than joy. Our message? Parenting is filled with opportunities to learn, grow, and have fun. In fact, the more you can recognize and let go of needless worries and guilt, the more you'll enjoy being a parent. This is want we want for you.

Letting Go

There are so many reasons parents can feel anxious and self-critical. For starters, parenting really is a big responsibility, and comes with little training and many demands. Once the excitement, attention, and congratulations around the new baby subside, the scary realization sets in that we are "It." This helpless infant is completely dependent on us. Then, just as we get the hang of being the one in charge, a new reality emerges. This once helpless child now has his own voice and ideas about how things should be. He doesn't need us in that same way and wants to take more and more control of his life. In fact, his healthy development and self-esteem depend on our gradual and wise relinquishing of control and responsibility for his care and well-being. From feeding himself to budgeting his own money, we become less of the primary "it," and more of a secondary support.

> *It was helpful for Jackson to be reminded that some of his perceived responsibility for his eleven-year-old son, Jera, was no longer necessary or appropriate. As he relaxed his hold, his son was free to meet new challenges and take more responsibility for himself. It wasn't easy for Jackson to watch when Jera struggled with frustration, but he got better at knowing when intervention or help was really necessary. Jackson no longer has to carry the full weight of Jera's happiness*

and well-being on his own shoulders. Even better, he gets to enjoy the satisfaction of watching Jera blossom and feel good about his accomplishments.

On Being a "Good Enough" Parent

There is another reason we, as parents, might feel overwhelmed and inadequate. We hold unrealistic expectations about what it means to be a good parent. For nine months we anticipate, dream, form promises, and envision the kind of parents we want to be. We also embrace an amazing faith that we can be these remarkable parents. We won't yell like our father did or be impatient like our mother. Our children will be respectful and not have temper tantrums in restaurants. Then, our conjured visions clash with the realities of parenting a real child. When every effort to comfort our screaming toddler, reason with our four-year-old, or have our teenager complete her homework fails, we feel a sense of failure or inadequacy.

Every time your expectations of yourself as a parent fall short, we want you to remember this mantra:

Your best is usually good enough.

There is no way to parent and not make mistakes, lose your cool, or forget your promises to yourself. All you can do is your best, for that day or that circumstance. Just as we told Jackson that he did not need to feel total responsibility for every aspect of his child's present and future life, he and you do not need to feel guilty because you aren't always the parent you want to be. In truth, even if we could do everything just right and meet our children's every need, it would not be in their best interest. It's actually a perfect system that parents are human and make mistakes. Adversity is a part of every life, so it follows that frustration and struggle, in manageable doses, provide children with practice. Challenge forces them to reach inside to find their own resources for comfort, problem solving, and growth.

When Zara's stressed and allergic mom yelled "Absolutely not!" in response to Zara's "Can I keep the stray dog?" plea, Zara was left on the doorstep with the dog. After a good cry, Zara called some friends until one's mom agreed to foster the dog while Zara promised to find a home or local rescue center.

A final word about being a good-enough parent: Kids are resilient and they are also forgiving. This is something we can learn from *them*. When we bring a light, forgiving heart to our mistakes, it frees us to enjoy our children and the experiences of parenting.

Think Lighthearted

As the parent, have you noticed that you're the mood setter in your home? Children tend to pick up your attitude and energy. When parents create and encourage an atmosphere of lightness, then family jokes, mirth, and friendly banter happen spontaneously. Laughter creates happy memories, and happy memories build strong bonds. A compassionate smile or a conspiratorial wink on your part can carry enough power to swiftly shift a mood or defuse a conflict. When you are looking for ways to infuse your parenting with lightness and fun, here are some ideas to get your creativity flowing.

- When spirits are low, have an unbirthday party.

- When cabin fever sets in, round up the whole family for a sport or game you don't usually do. Take the kids bowling or to a square dance or a climbing wall.

- When you find yourself feeling stressed-out and at the end of your rope, picture a miniature you sitting inside you, smiling contentedly. Put him/her in a lotus position if that helps. Tune into him or her and see if it doesn't lighten your mood.

- When your child is really bugging you, imagine squirting him with Silly String.

- When feathers are a bit ruffled, defuse tension without being rude. Get creative. Remember a funny story, use self-deprecating humor, or try the tickle game.

- For a truly democratic household, once a week have the kids make dinner. You must eat it, no matter what. (Draw the line at mud pies.)

- Feeling underappreciated? Don't wait for Mother's Day or Father's Day to declare, "Appreciate Mom or Dad Day."

- When you need a dose of magic to brighten your day, build fairy houses or troll bridges with your child.

- When things feel dull or boring, exercise your creativity together. Visit the thrift store for dress-up costumes or use cardboard boxes to create play houses, hamster houses, castles, or ships.

- Physical activity creates positive energy. Get moving together. Sing, dance, do yoga, or play Wii together.

- À la Mary Poppins and Barney, make a game out of chores—e.g., clean-up relay races or crazy walks while setting the table, or create a fantasy context like pretending the bathroom you are cleaning is in the Taj Mahal.

- Look over the activities in your Parenting Plan. Tweak them to ensure that you include things that are enjoyable and fulfilling for you too.

- If you are at a loss, watch your child. Children naturally use their imaginations and creativity to make their own fun.

Parents' Stories

In our personal experience and in our workshops, we have learned that parents are the best help and support for other parents. Fresh perspectives, creative solutions, reality checks, and shared experiences are immensely valuable for all of us. That's why, at the end of workshops when we come to this part, we ask parents to tell their stories about finding balance and enjoyment in their parenting. We want to know what helped each of them cultivate a light heart, discover a new perspective, relax more, worry less, or enjoy the opportunities parenting opens up. Here are some of their stories.

- **Josie: Remembering to take care of me too.** Josie is a single mom with a boy and a girl. She works part-time and has full custody.

  Doing the exercises in Chapter 2 reminded me how much I used to love ice-skating. One afternoon while the three of us were watching an ice-skating event on TV, I told them how I loved to skate years ago, and suggested we all try it. I found a rink not too far away, and signed us all up for lessons. I don't know what was more fun—whizzing around on the ice again, watching the glee on my two kids' faces as they learned to balance and glide, or having them say I skated just like the teacher. Resentment of having no life other than being their mom tends to sneak up on me, so I must remember how nice it felt that day to do something for myself, and how much fun we all had.

- **Paul: Slow down and open to your experience.** Paul works at home and cares for three-year-old Leroy; Ann works outside the home.

  Leroy is a laid-back kid, so it's easy to give him something to do while I work on the computer or make calls. I take a few moments here and there to get him started with something, and then, back to my work. So often I feel pressured and distracted because I'm trying to do two things at once, and it seems nothing gets done well. Hearing other parents talk about all they noticed and learned while observing their children encouraged me to pay more attention. The other day I set my work aside and decided to watch Leroy play. It was a nice spring day so we went outside. Leroy ran around some and then settled on the patio where he began gently picking up small ants and carrying them to their hole in between the patio stones. As I watched, I thought back to when I was small and watched spiders and ants much like Leroy. His patience and gentleness were amazing, and I noticed he was talking to the ants as he moved them about. After a while, I just got up and joined him. We watched the ants together and speculated about what their house might look like or how far they traveled. Time went by. I felt calm and happy and really there with Leroy. When I did get back to work I was more productive than I had been in weeks, and more relaxed. This was a good lesson for me. Work is important, but being a father feels great. When I feel good about myself and can relax, everything else flows better.

- **Suzanne: Things aren't inherently bad or good; it's how you frame them.** Suzanne and Dan have a ten-year-old daughter, Dana.

Dana was born with many physical and emotional challenges, and parenting her isn't easy. She still tantrums often and needs a lot of assistance and soothing. Dan is so present and involved, but I still struggle with my feelings. Lately, talking with Dan about the idea of reframing and perspective has launched me on a helpful course. I am becoming better and better at viewing my parenting job as creative and loving rather than tedious and burdensome. For example, I have to cut Dana's food into small pieces and make sure she drinks water in between bites. It gets somewhat tedious. A week or so ago I decided to tell myself one good thing about myself and my life with each slice of chicken I cut. That felt pretty good. I then started to get more creative in how I cut the pieces, using different shapes and sizes. Dana noticed this, and now we have a game—she tries to guess what shape I am cutting her lunch sandwich into or how many pieces the banana ends up in. I can't keep this up throughout the day, but it helps us to laugh more and eases some stress. Hopefully, I can find more ways to create enjoyment in our day-to-day care routines.

● **Evelyn: Experiencing the magic of creativity and humor.** Evelyn and Joe have children ages twelve and thirteen.

Michael was one of those kids who could play outside all day and half the night. During the summer with the long days, he consistently forgot about our dinner hour. Many nights, I would have to go around the neighborhood calling for Mike while dinner and everyone else waited. Reminders didn't help, and even though he had a watch, he forgot to look at it. I warned him I was running out of patience, but he continued to be lax. Finally, one evening I decided to show him I meant business AND have a little fun. I got Michael's band trumpet and headed for the front yard. I blew that trumpet long and badly. Michael was embarrassed and more than a little incredulous. But he got pretty good about his curfew after that. Amazing how a little humor and creative problem solving cured his "parent deafness." I still giggle thinking about it. I'm sure he'll laugh about it too—when he's older!

- **Monique: Letting go of control and giving responsibility.** She raises eight-year-old Robert by herself.

  When I reflected on the idea of enjoying my parenting more, I realized I was coming home from work each day dreading our evening routine—fixing dinner, the inevitable homework battles, the bath Robert never wants to leave, and bed he never wants to go to. Although I said independence was a parenting priority, I felt like I needed to control the routine if it was all going to get done. Then, something inside me said I had to loosen my hold if this was going to get any better. Last weekend I decided to give some of the control to Robert. I set the bedtime knowing there was early soccer practice in the morning. For the rest of the weekend he could set his own schedule and the way he wanted to do his homework and chores—as long as he was in bed by 8:00 and everything got done. We used a whiteboard to write his to-do list so he could erase each task as he finished it. I can't say it was easy for me, but Robert did great, and was quite proud of his empty whiteboard. It was a good start, so I'm hopeful that our weekday evenings can be less stressful.

- **Susan: Hearing and heeding the voices of many.** One dad, one mom, and four children, ages seven, nine, thirteen, and fifteen.

  Peter and I finished Part II and felt kind of overwhelmed with all the individual needs and voices we were trying to consider in our large family. We talked about a few things and came up with this idea: Everyone was invited to bring one family-related pet peeve to a meeting. We would listen to each other and then try for one month to honor each person's request. I didn't want to be interrupted on the phone.

Peter wanted the children to stop what they were doing long enough to say hello when he came home from work. John (the oldest) wanted his sisters to stop eavesdropping on his phone calls and asking questions about his girlfriends. Suzie hated that her chores were always "girl's work," and wanted her brother to get those jobs sometimes. Nancy wanted <u>everyone</u> to stop teasing her about how much she talked, and Cindy (the baby) wanted us to stop calling and treating her like "the baby." I was surprised by what some of the children said bothered them, and it opened the door to some interesting conversations. We had fun with this and saw how easily unconscious, even hurtful behaviors develop in a family setting. I think we also got to see each other a little differently. I felt really proud of all of us!

● **James: Seeing your child with an open heart and mind.** Bobbie and James have two daughters, each one very much an individual.

It always amazes me how different each of my daughters is. Jesse is the older one. Bright, organized, and focused, with a commonsense approach to life. She's ambitious but in a reserved way. I realize she and I share that easy-going temperament and first child maturity. Focusing on her as an individual, I learned that I have to make a point to ask for her opinion and not always assume she sees things as I do. When I do, I am often surprised and humbled by her responses. Then there's Caryn, the younger one. Sometimes I wonder where she came from—we are so different. She's very sensitive and quite intense. Her sensitive nature sometimes feels finicky to me, and her intense feelings and emotions often have us all bracing ourselves. It can be hard for me but I have really come to appreciate her passion. I am so enchanted by both of my daughters and love watching how they put their imprint on their worlds.

> **TRY THIS:** *Now share a story that might help another parent. It might be about a new perspective you've gained, a realization of being good enough, or a way you found to enjoy parenting more.*

In the continued spirit of sharing, we thought we would end with two stories from our own parenting experiences.

● **Joan: Some thoughts about giving.**

Coming from a large family with a mother who unconditionally gave to all of us, I had an angry reaction the first (and last) time I read Megan Shel Silverstein's The Giving Tree. *My reaction caught me by surprise. (Lest I receive angry letters from Shel Silverstein fans, I will just add that Megan loved Shel Silverstein's poetry and I read it to her often.)*

Briefly, it is the story/parable of a tree that lovingly and unconditionally gives, and a boy who receives the tree's gifts only to come back and ask for more. As the boy grows into a man, he continues to ask—and the tree continues to lovingly give—until only a stump remains of the once beautiful tree. The tree serenely accepts that the love and giving is one-sided.

My unexpectedly negative response caused me to pause and consider why. I spent a lot of time thinking about the connection between love and giving, the distinction between indulgence and value, and the parent-child relationship I wanted with Megan. I realized what bothered me most about the story was that the loving sacrifices the tree made never provided any lasting pleasure or satisfaction for the boy or the man—or gratitude from him. The tree's sacrifice and gifts were wasted and served no one.

We give to our children because we love them. The Giving Tree *helped me realize that not all giving is loving, or even supportive. Our giving deserves thoughtful consideration about its purpose and value.*

● **Sheila: On making family memories.**

In the remake of the movie The Parent Trap *(which my then eight-year-old daughter, Marika, watched endlessly), there's a scene where the American granddaughter, upon first meeting her British grandfather, steps up to purposefully sniff his jacket. He asks what she is doing and she replies, "Making memories." Then, with each sniff, she describes his scent of tobacco, peppermint, etc. and explains that, wherever she is, these smells will remind her of him and the warm connection she feels with him.*

Before having children, I hardly considered the depth of connection that's created by "making memories" together—how these memories link us, for better or worse, deeply in our conscious and unconscious minds. Birthday gift-opening rituals and bedtime rituals; dress-up plays and high school shows; choosing our bunny and burying our dog; making snow-and-maple-syrup "ice cream"; and fixing favorite dishes for special days. It's our collection of memories that ties us and builds the story of our family—its identity and culture.

When the girls were little, we made a book called, The Azoff Book of Quotations. *Colorful figures, scribbles, and a six-year-old's lettering spelled out the funny expressions and nicknames that became part of our daily vocabulary: "bluebazzies" for blueberries, "where the minnows kiss your legs" for our swimming hole, and "I'm just going to nap, NOT SLEEP!" This bookmaking was our family's first time stepping back and seeing the unfolding of our story together. It was a moment when I experienced our bond as citizens of this land of Azoff—creating our language, culture, and history together—and felt how happy it made me to belong to this clan.*

Families, whatever size or configuration, without effort or awareness, create their independent island, the culture and people to which they belong.

Our family culture includes a lot of singing. Certain songs remind us of experiences we shared. Through the twenty-four years of being a family, as siblings shift between rivalry and alliance and children push away and come back around, our sense of family remains a constant, a base. I strive to create at least some time each year when we all have a vacation or adventure together: building memories. Otherwise, I mostly get to sit back and observe Ariel and Marika create their independent lives. I feel so deeply moved when one of them reaches out to touch down or dip into this well of family to nourish or ground them. Like a desire to come home and be nurtured for a weekend, or to light holiday candles together, across the ocean, via Skype. Standing at the kitchen sink during Thanksgiving weekend, when both daughters were home, I listened to them laughing and making music in the adjoining room. I again felt so happy and appreciative of this unit I'm a part of, recognizing now that, as we share a song, we revisit and revise our family history—one memory at a time.

Our intention for this book was to create a process that would ultimately help you, the parent, trust yourself. Children don't come with owners' manuals, and parents often tell us that they feel as if they don't know what they're doing. But now that you've worked through these chapters, you know a great deal more, don't you? You've learned about your own needs and traits, discovered facets of your child you may not have considered before, and clarified your parenting intentions. Going forward, every time you make a parenting decision, you can now trust yourself, knowing that your decisions aren't random, but are based on your voice, your child, and your vision.

Parenting requires a tremendous amount of your energy and involvement, but it also gives back a lot. Don't lose sight of how much you are influencing a young life, but also what you're learning and gaining in return as a result of everything you put into parenting. As one mother told us, "having a child opened my heart and taught me new truths about myself and life's purpose."

CHAPTER *12* TAKE-AWAYS

- *No parent always feels joyful, confident, and competent in their parenting.*

- *The complexities of parenting are compounded by everything from our own level of preparedness to the challenge of gradually letting go of control.*

- *Parents are usually "good enough." Missteps, mistakes, confusion, and frustration are expected and actually instructive for our children in manageable doses.*

- *When we accept our inevitable shortfalls, it frees us to laugh at ourselves and enjoy our parenting more.*

- *We give ourselves a wonderful gift when we can lighten the responsibility we feel to be the perfect or near-perfect parent.*

- *Parenting offers opportunities for us to expand our ways of feeling, seeing, and growing, like no other experience in our life.*

My Notes and Questions

_____

_____

_____

_____

_____

_____

_____

_____

_____

_____

_____

_____

_____

_____

_____

_____

_____

_____

_____

_____

_____

_____

_____

_____

_____

_____

_____

Appendix
1

Parents' Strategies
for Accommodating Their
Child's Temperament

n Chapter 6, you learned about your child's temperament traits, and
read examples of real-life children whose parents did the same exercise
as you. Their stories are in the assessment exercise examples, pages 96–
106. But how did these parents learn to deal with their children's temperament traits? We thought it would be helpful, maybe even inspiring for you
to see the strategies these parents came up with, using what they learned
from the *Parenting In Your Own Voice* process.

ACTIVITY LEVEL

Refers to the amount of physical movement that is typically exerted by the child. How much energy needs to be released?

Extremely active behavior:	Quiet/inactive behavior:
Play is full of movement	Play is more sedentary
Sleeps all over the bed	Sleeps in one place
Sitting for short dinner is difficult	Can sit through a long dinner
Has trouble sitting for any play	Can sit for long periods of play
Moves/walks as thinks/learns	Sits quietly when thinking/learning
More emotion, more activity	Emotion not physically demonstrated
Body parts move while sitting	Body is still while sitting

Examples

JACKSON: Jackson constantly needs to move. School is extremely challenging because it requires too much quiet sitting. At home, even when he's sitting, he isn't still—some part of his body is always in motion. After school he needs to have a great deal of physical activity or he will be too revved up to fall asleep. He has difficulty sitting still long enough to finish homework carefully, and he has never fallen asleep easily.

> *Parenting strategy:* Physical outlets for his energy are the best medicine for Jackson. With him, we have tried to figure out healthy ways he can use his energy. Before school, he makes some money walking neighbors' dogs. One good thing about being in a large high school is that he often has to walk a distance from class to class. At lunch and after school he runs track, plays basketball, or takes a tennis lesson. When it comes to homework, he gets overwhelmed just reading the assignments he has to complete, so we

break things down for him with short work periods marked by frequent, brief breaks to get up and move around. Then we show him what he's accomplished and what's next on his list. We try to be positive and encouraging. It seems to be helping. He's getting his homework done with much less stress. Practicing breathing techniques he's learned from a meditation program is helping Jackson to sleep better. Another parent told us about a biofeedback computer program their daughter has been using that helps her to sleep.

TROY: Whenever something with wheels is available, Troy is riding it, chasing it, or playing with it. At school he can sit and work as long as there is a recess or gym break so he can run and play. After school he likes to have some time to ride his bike or play outside, but then he will come in and do his homework straight through. Before bed there is usually some quiet activity and little drama about going to bed.

Parenting strategy: It's best for Troy to do something physical each day—a bike ride, the trampoline. During a stretch of rainy days, he and his friends created an obstacle course in the basement. After a few hours of action, he does best with some time to eat and curl up with a book or get involved in a project.

LUCY: Lucy seems to be more of a thinker than a doer. If you bring a toy to her, she gladly plays with it, but would not likely get it on her own. If she doesn't have a toy, she sits and looks around, takes in her surroundings, or finds something nearby to explore. Even after learning to walk, she preferred to be carried and usually gravitated to the sandbox rather than the slides, swings, or jungle gym. It is also rather amazing how long she can sit in a restaurant without getting antsy.

Parenting strategy: We've learned to set aside extra time for Lucy since she tends to go at a slower pace. Every day we arrange some sort of outing to get her up and moving—swimming with a friend, a picnic, etc. We've encouraged her exuberant, high-energy older sister to invite Lucy along on some of her adventures. Lucy usually finds anything her older sister does enticing.

REGULARITY

Refers to the degree of predictability that accompanies a child's biological functions.

Regularity:	Irregularity:
Sleep patterns follow a schedule	Sleep patterns erratic
Feels hungry at consistent times	Hunger patterns erratic
Eats a predictable amount of food	Food intake may vary a lot
Elimination is predictable	Elimination erratic

Examples

MAX: Max has always relied on a stable daily rhythm. He's up early, uses the bathroom three times a day like clockwork, and never stays up much past 11. With some adjustments, he can be flexible, but he seems to be at his best within his schedule. (When he was a baby, other parents envied the predictability of our days and nights.) Even now, at fifteen years old, he is looking for those three meals a day at around the same time. Though he goes to sleep a lot later, he still needs his eight hours or he's a cranky mess.

Parenting strategy: For Max, knowing about his own rhythms makes everything better for everyone. For example, if he goes out for the day and brings along food so he can eat at his usual time, he finds his mood and energy level are much better. When he was young we were able to avoid many unpleasant situations by keeping him as close to his usual schedule as possible. There wasn't much guesswork since his needs were so predictable.

BERNADETTE: Bernadette loves to eat. She goes along with the family's schedule, three meals a day with a midmorning and mid-afternoon snack. Her daily rhythms are fairly regular, but you can't set your watch by her. Sometimes she's asleep by 7, sometimes 8.

Parenting strategy: Because our rhythms are so in sync, no strategies or accommodations have been needed.

FULVIA: Fulvia greets each day anew. Some days she's ravenous and can eat throughout the day. Other days she hardly touches a morsel. Nap times and bedtimes are equally different. To have any routine ourselves, we must put her to bed at a certain time and accept that she may stay awake in her room.

Parenting strategy: Accepting Fulvia's rhythms and taking care of our own needs has made a huge difference in our household. Knowing that her sleep patterns won't always be predictable, we hire a babysitter whenever we must keep to a schedule. We've set a time for Fulvia to go to bed and created a bedtime routine. If she doesn't go right to sleep, we know she's safe in her bed with a book and her stuffed animals. She can sit with us for a meal without eating much if she's not hungry. We accommodate her need for flexibility of routines by allowing her to eat when she *is* hungry.

INITIAL REACTION TO NEW SITUATIONS

Refers to the child's response when introduced to a new situation or experience.

Withdraws/stands back:	Approaches/jumps in:
Cries when sees a stranger	Easily goes to a stranger
Will not accept a substitute toy	Will accept a substitute toy at bedtime
Only likes certain familiar food	Readily accepts a new food
Hesitates or refuses to join play	Starts playing right away at a party

Examples

JASON: We were so unsure how to handle Jason in social situations. He's bright and likes people, but when we take him to a party or to the playground, he clings to my leg. He stands there watching for what feels like forever, and then (just around the time to leave) tentatively joins in. He's like that with food, too. We have to offer a new food several times before he'll try it.

> *Parenting strategy:* We've learned to plan ahead. When we go to new places, we go early to give Jason time to acclimate. It makes a world of difference. If he has time to get to know the other kids, he will join them more readily and we all have a much better time. In situations we don't anticipate, we talk to him a lot and push a little, and then let him find his comfort zone, accepting that it may not happen soon. The other day we went to a new restaurant. Though we made sure the menu included something he will eat, we encouraged him to try something new.

FRANCISCO: Francisco really likes to go places and meet new people, but you wouldn't always know it. For example, when a friend's child came running up to him yelling hello while grabbing his hand to show him a game she was excited about, he stopped dead in his tracks and turned to me with a look of desperation on his face. It took a little while for him to warm up to her after that—but he did. The other day we took him to a Japanese restaurant and he had a ball trying the dumplings and tempura dishes. He even tried to use the chopsticks.

> *Parenting strategy:* If you approach Francisco calmly with anything new or unexpected, he generally stays pretty open. He's typically fine with new kids on the playground, but if the new child is overpowering or intrusive, Francisco backs up and withdraws. At these times, we help him to assert his need for some space or time, giving him words like, "I don't want to play right now." This helps him feel like he has some control—and then he's less overwhelmed.

MELANIE: Melanie has always been a people person. At school, she introduces herself to the new kid or joins the volleyball game on the playground even when she knows no other player. She loves to travel. You could put her in a different bed each night or in a new situation every day and she would be just fine. It's a stark contrast to me, her dad, who feels best staying close to my things and familiar surroundings.

> *Parenting strategy:* I do have to teach Melanie about observing people and not trusting just anyone. Giving her guidance about safety and maintaining her boundaries without stifling her enthusiasm is key. For example, asking questions like, "Who will be driving?" and "Will there be adults on this campout?" are important. She may roll her eyes, but she answers.

ADAPTABILITY

Refers to the amount of time/energy it takes for the child to adjust to change (assuming they can).

Does not adapt readily:	Adapts readily:
Not easily able to change the usual with something different	Can easily change a bed or usual chair
Needs preparation for new caregiver	New caregiver presents little adjustment
Transition to new activity difficult	Moves readily from one activity to another
Difficulty with different clothing	Change-of-season clothing no issue
Moving to different classes hard	Changes classrooms without a problem

Examples

ALYSSA: Shopping for clothes is supposed to be a fun mother-daughter experience. Not for Alyssa and me. She has such a hard time accepting anything new or different. Whether it's a new coat, a new family car, or even a piece of furniture, each experience is met with anger and upset. She'd much rather wear the old coat she's outgrown. Changes are just hard.

> *Parenting strategy:* A few times we really planned ahead and bought the same shirt in two sizes so Alyssa would grow into the second one without having to shop again. That really worked well. When changes are coming, we give her advanced warning, empathize with how hard this can be for her, and lend support in getting her used to the idea. There may still be a meltdown. Lately, we notice she is working to find her own ways to cope with changes.

WAYNE: Wayne takes a little while to switch gears. When we go to his grandparents' house, he needs me there with him for the first hour or so. Then I can leave and he's fine. If we go back the very next day, he still needs me there for a few minutes before he'll say, "Bye, Ma."

Parenting strategy: We don't expect Wayne to accept changes right away. We know he needs a little time to adapt. Given that time, he's generally fine. For example, we took him camping for the first time. He was really uncomfortable being in the tent, worrying about bugs and bears. None of us got a lot of sleep, but we let him know we weren't leaving until the ten days were up. We also reminded him that he does, eventually, get used to things. He loved the fires and the swimming, and after several nights, he finally began to feel comfortable and was able to fall asleep.

NATE: Nate is so flexible. What a break. Being the youngest of four children, it really helps that he can go with the flow. When I have to run to school for one of his brothers, or take his grandfather to an appointment, he has to be left at a friend's or with a babysitter. If it's a new sitter or I wake him from his nap to take him, he complains for a few minutes, but then he quickly adjusts, and goes with a smile. Nate came into the world like this. We can't take any credit.

Parenting strategy: With a son like Nate, we found we need to encourage him to say what HE wants when he's with his brothers or it's always their way. We want him to practice asserting himself so that others don't take advantage of his easy nature. It is important to his mom that he tunes into his own interests and feelings, which is not always easy for a child who is just as happy to go along with things.

PREDOMINANT MOOD

Refers to the prevalent mood that a child expresses throughout the day—how they view the world in general.

Sees the glass as half empty:	Sees the glass as half full:
Serious, wary of people, fussy	Cheerful, friendly, easy to please
Cries often over seemingly small things	Takes a lot to bring them to tears
Tends to see the negative/problems in a situation	Tends to see positive in a situation
Holds on to bad feelings	Fusses briefly and moves on
World is often frightening	Acts as if the world is a safe place

Examples

APRIL: When my self-esteem was tied to April's responses to me or my attempts to make her smile, I felt quite dejected. Then I stepped back and saw that she responded to everyone and everything similarly. She's very touchy and can be somewhat of a curmudgeon. When other toddlers laugh, she frowns. From her point of view, the glass is usually half empty. Exuberant, gleeful responses? They're just not her way.

> *Parenting strategy:* April's the kind of child who needs tender loving care and lots of reassurance. She can also use some pointers sometimes on how to be a more inviting playmate, if given in a supportive, noncritical way. It's important not to take her reactions personally and to especially stay tuned for the little smiles of appreciation that come once in awhile. They mean the world.

HERNAN: Hernan gets upset when he's uncomfortable or frustrated. If he hasn't gotten enough sleep and has lots of schoolwork, he may feel sad and burdened and sound a bit like Eeyore. Usually, though, Hernan is cheerful and upbeat. He loves to joke and make his sisters laugh and can brighten everyone's mood.

> *Parenting strategy:* When he's rested and not entrenched in his reaction yet, a few words of encouragement or a positive attitude can shake Hernan out of his negative stance. He will even laugh at himself once in awhile. Allowing him to express his different moods and talking about what brings him down sometimes helps. He has become more aware of the things that cause him stress.

DEAN: The word *enthusiastic* best describes Dean. Since he was in preschool, he's seemed to find the world to be a very exciting and wonderful place. Of course he gets upset at times, but he doesn't stay upset for very long. He laughs aloud a lot, even if he's reading something funny to himself. His whole being smiles.

> *Parenting strategy:* Dean really takes the best from most situations. One day we went on an outing to the park and the playground equipment had been painted and was closed off. He loves the slide and swings and was quite frustrated—for a minute or two. Then he found some stones to pitch into a puddle, which led to a discovery of a frog and some snails, which was so exciting that he didn't look back. We do have to explain to Dean that not everyone sees things in a positive light in order to help him understand other people's feelings (like why his friend cried about the playground).

PERSISTENCE

Refers to the child's ability to let go of an activity or feeling.

Totally determined:	Low persistence:
Will not let go of what they want	Can be easily redirected or distracted
Appears "locked in" and rigid	Feelings pass quickly
Holds on to feelings (this might be the child who will not stop crying)	Accepts, with minimum fuss, when told "no"
Must finish an activity they choose	Can let go of an unfinished activity
Continues when extremely frustrated	Backs away from a frustrating activity
Never changes their mind	Mind can be changed easily
Never wears what they do not like	Can be cajoled into wearing something they do not love

Examples

WILLIE: Willie came into the world singing, "I'll do it my way." After running through the labels Oppositional, Defiant, Unreasonable, and Willful, we've come to realize that Focused, capital "F," best describes Willie. Whether he's trying a new sport or a crossword puzzle, he keeps at it. In fact, trying to get him to stop is excruciatingly difficult. When he sets his mind to something, a certain food or pair of sneakers, it's very hard to get him to accept an alternative or take no for an answer.

> *Parenting strategy:* One thing that helps Willie is to problem solve ahead of time. We might discuss how he can best handle having to leave his TV show before it ends, or what he will do when we shop for sneakers he needs for gym if they don't have the purple high

tops. He can often come up with some good ideas that work. If only life's changes and disappointments always provided advanced warning. Also, as he gets older, when he is feeling good and we are just chatting, we talk about this tendency of his, the positive and negative aspects. Now I can tell him when he's getting stuck on something and needs to move on. Sometimes this is helpful. Other times he's too entrenched in his response and needs time to get through it.

BRIELLE: Brielle can concentrate on her schoolwork when it's interesting OR when she has to prepare for a test. If distracted by a phone call or her brother, she can usually get right back to it. If she doesn't understand something, she tends to ask myself or her teacher to explain it to her rather than to go over it and over it until she gets it. When she gets upset about what her boyfriend said or if I set some limit she doesn't like, it's a little difficult for her to let the feelings go. But she still takes care of her responsibilities and doesn't get completely sidetracked.

Parenting strategy: The best we can do to support Brielle is to be available when she needs to figure something out or discuss difficult feelings. She has come to know when to ask us to talk. As a younger child, when an activity or assignment was challenging, she just needed a little guidance to avoid too much frustration, along with some encouragement to persevere. This seemed to be the best recipe.

MARYANN: MaryAnn has no stick-to-it-tiveness. Though she may get engrossed in something, in comes her sister or a friend, and she drops everything to join them. If the puzzle or math question becomes challenging, she gives up quickly. She's certainly smart enough to figure things out if she would persevere. On the other hand, she's one who can truly "go with the flow." If plans change, or if she has to settle for a different flavor ice cream, whatever it is, she's accepting and moves on quickly.

> *Parenting strategy:* We find that we have to stay with MaryAnn to help her to persevere. If we work on the difficult math problem with her, or refocus her to her chores when her sister walks by, she'll stay with things a bit longer. Often, just being near her and offering soothing encouragement can help her to face a challenge. The excitement of success helps her to continue. But she still needs the support and reminders to stick with her own choices, responsibilities, and ideas rather than go along with the group.

PERCEPTIVENESS / DISTRACTIBILITY

Refers to the degree a child's focus is interrupted by outside stimuli (sound, smell, movement, etc.)

Perceives all:	Barely notices:
Hears and sees everything, and often reacts to that stimuli	Often unaware of peripheral stimuli/sights
Task might get completed, but it takes longer with distractions	Can stay on task when distractions are present
Keenly aware of emotions and stress	May be unaware of other people's emotions
Difficulty with multiple instructions	Remembers multiple instructions

Examples

FARRELL: Farrell is drawn to everything around him. As he eats his chicken nuggets at the dinner table, he is reaching over to grab his brother's fries. In a flash, he might jump up from the table to look for the ambulance he hears down the street. Ask him to go inside and get his shoes, and ten minutes later you see him completing a puzzle on the table in the hallway. On the other hand, there's little he misses. He reads the annoyed expression on your face and responds before you say a word; he knows his mother's approaching from the smell of her perfume and can identify most birds from their song.

> *Parenting strategy:* Farrell is so easily distracted we have prepared a quiet place for him to work. We encourage projects or chores that can be completed within a short time frame so he can accomplish things and feel good about them, and we keep his sister and brother away from him until he is finished. With people's tendency to lose their patience with Farrell, it's tricky to help him stay on track without making him feel bad. He's such a perceptive child. We focus on the plus side of being as aware of things as he is. For example, we tend to rely on him to let us know what's going on with his brother when we're stumped. The other day the baby was screaming and we couldn't figure out why. Farrell told us the light was on over the crib shining right into Jason's eyes. He was right.

HARRIS: Harris loves to get immersed in a puzzle or play with his cars and trucks. If he's engrossed in something, there is not much that distracts him. When his interest wanes, he'll leave his cars to see what cartoon his sister is watching or follow the smell of cookies baking in the kitchen. Most of the time he reads his sister or me well enough to know when to back off.

> *Parenting strategy:* Harris doesn't need a lot of assistance. He reads cues pretty well and can stay focused on things when he wants or needs to. Sometimes, we have to remind him to clean up or get his jacket.

MAY: May is a whiz at taking care of business. She gets home from school, does her homework, then her chores, and can enjoy her TV program before bed. If you ask her to get something done, you can usually be assured that she'll do it, regardless of what's going on around her. Being so focused on a task to the exclusion of all else means she's not paying attention to the subtleties around her, such as a needy friend or a colorful sky.

> *Parenting strategy:* Now that she is getting old enough, we try to help May be more sensitive to other people's feelings. When someone is upset with her and she doesn't know why, we use these opportunities to help her understand what the other person may be experiencing. When her sister asks her a question and she ignores her, we encourage her sister to wait until May is finished with her activity and then ask. While we appreciate her incredible ability to tune in to the details of what she is focused on, we often bring her attention to other things around her to enrich and enliven her experience, like the hummingbird next to us on the porch.

INTENSITY

Refers to the child's depth of emotional reaction. What passion and energy do they bring?

Powerful reaction:	Mild reaction:
Excitement is exuberant and animated	Excitement is controlled with a smile
Wailing	Small crying/whimpering
Drama queen	Stoic
Easily frustrated	Handles frustration

Examples

ABIGAIL: It was great to hear my daughter's kindergarten teacher tell me, with loving appreciation, "I've never met a child who feels her feelings as strongly as Abigail." The intensity of her tears when we separated was only equal to her gleeful laughter when she played with a puppy, or her overwhelming frustration when she couldn't tie her shoe. She reacts passionately to most of life.

> *Parenting strategy:* Helping Abigail to navigate her emotional ups and downs is part of parenting her. A lot of empathy and listening seems to work best. Then, once she's calm, she can ask for help figuring things out if she needs it. She often does well on her own, once she's processed her reactions, as she has a good understanding of people. Knowing she needs to express things in a big way helps us not to overreact. As she gets older, it will be important for her to learn that her initial reactions are intense. The next step will be to help her to learn strategies to moderate her responses and calm down enough to think clearly.

MAGGIE: Maggie is a bubbly child. Her laugh is contagious. For the most part, she is even tempered and without much drama, although you have to know her well to read some of her moods. When she's sad or afraid she will get quiet, but make her angry and she'll stomp off with great fanfare, loudly declaring she needs to be alone.

> *Parenting strategy:* While respecting her desire to be alone, we also try to help Maggie express her anger more productively, in words and discussion. If we ask her how she's feeling when she's quiet and looks upset, she can usually tell us and talk about things. She just needs to be drawn out a bit at times.

RICHIE: Richie is so smart and curious, even at eight years old. His sense of humor is intelligent and somewhat low key, and it's often hard to read his feelings because his reactions are so subtle. His friends appreciate his good ideas for games to play, and he's never competitive with them. For his last birthday, he said he really wanted a stapler for his gift—one of those little red ones with the small staples. When he opened his present, he smiled and said "Thanks!" and went off to do some stapling.

> *Parenting strategy:* You can't need enthusiastic reactions with a kid like Richie. We know he really appreciates things, he just doesn't show his feelings in a big way. Since he doesn't show his frustration or upset much, we make a point of drawing him out, asking him about his reactions to situations. Often, we find that he does have a feeling or opinion and he comes alive when talking about it.

SENSITIVITY

Refers to the awareness and reaction a child has to differences in sensory stimuli—*The Princess and the Pea* syndrome.

Very sensitive:	Tolerant:
Sleep interrupted by noise or light	Sleeps through noise or light
Hypersensitive to textiles, clothing tags, odors, textures	Indifferent to the way things feel or smell
Very fussy eater	Eats most anything
Hypersensitive to tension	Minimally affected by tension

Examples

MICHAEL: Michael will only wear cotton shirts with an open neck, nothing too tight, and he changes his clothing at least twice a day. His diet is limited to meat and potatoes—more specifically, hamburgers, fried chicken, and french fries. The only green thing he'll consume are string beans. It drives him crazy if there's a hint of static on the radio or if the lights are too glaring, and he can smell things the dog barely notices. What a kid. With his sensitivity, he really can appreciate a beautiful piece of music and the smell of freshly cut grass much more than most of us.

> *Parenting strategy:* Once I realized he wasn't trying to be difficult, but just reacting to his experience of things, I began to imagine how difficult it must be to be inside Michael's skin sometimes. While I try to ease him into tolerating a little more noise or odors, to help him get used to more stimulation, I also try to find fabrics that are comfortable for him. I try to be alert to the amount of stimuli he might encounter. He can express his limits more and more in words rather than just reacting, which is also helpful. As he gets older, we'll discuss his sensitivities and ways to increase his tolerance.

JANE: Jane is aware of sights and sounds around her but can tune things out when she needs to. She loves visitors, so when she hears the dog bark downstairs she comes running to see who is at the door. If she's playing with her girlfriend, the phone can ring and ring but she ignores it. She likes soft blankets and appreciates the smell of clean towels, but won't fuss if she has to wear her wool jacket that's a bit scratchy. She can't sleep with the light on, and she hates to have the sun in her eyes.

> *Parenting strategy:* We bought Jane a great pair of sunglasses. Her room has blinds and curtains to keep the light out, which help her fall asleep.

ARIEL: We were amazed when Ariel slept through the blasting of the cinder block wall on the back of our house. She could sleep through anything. As a first child, it was great that she didn't mind noise or lights or changes in her surroundings, since we often took her visiting family and friends on the weekends. These things just don't seem to faze her.

> *Parenting strategy:* As she gets older, we try to direct Ariel's attention to some of these sensations, like the loudness of her music, for instance, just to make her more aware.

Appendix
2

More about the Intelligences

I f there is a more loaded topic within the discussion of seeing our children than that of intelligence, we would be hard-pressed to find it. As much as we may want to distance ourselves from its importance to us as parents, doing so is often our biggest challenge. Learning more about the eight (plus one) intelligences can be extremely enlightening for parents as well as teachers.

Based on Howard Gardner's seminal book, *Frames of Mind*, we include here more detailed descriptions and examples of the eight intelligences he identified, as well as the ninth, Existential, to which he did not fully commit.

LINGUISTIC: This is certainly one of the primary intelligences that is predominately used in our educational system. It is our ability to use and understand language.

The verbal-linguistic child:

- Uses language effectively to influence, explain, question, or motivate.

- Thinks in words, not pictures.

- Uses language to help understand, reflect, or create visualizations.

- Has a curiosity about language.

- Is sensitive to the meanings, sounds, and rhythms of words.

Examples of verbal-linguistic intelligence:

- Enjoys books, and hearing and telling stories.

- Is interested in poetry and writing.

- Finds pleasure in humor as well as "twists" of the language.

- Enjoys solving crossword puzzles and riddles, and playing word games.

- Loves to talk.

LOGICAL-MATHEMATICAL: This is the second area of competence that is most often evaluated and valued in the school setting. It is reflected in our ability to use reason, logic, and numbers.

The logical-mathematical child:

- Shows an interest in numbers and quantity the way a linguistic child has an interest in words.

- Has a fascination with patterns, categories, and relationships.

- Has good spatial comprehension.

Examples of mathematical intelligence:

- Fascinated with cause and effect of the physical world—the "why" questions.

- Likes experiments and frequently thinks "What if?"

- Easily computes numbers in her head.

- Thinks in abstract concepts without images or words.

- Shows early ability to understand underlying concepts of math.

- Speculates on rules about the behavior of things based on her own observations.

- Needs things to be logical, for things to "add up."

- Loves dealing with abstraction.

- Exhibits excellent ability to estimate or consider probability.

- Shows interest in ordering or categorizing.

- Likes strategy games such as chess or cribbage.

MUSICAL: This is the ability to produce and appreciate music.

The musical-rhythmic child:

- Possesses keen auditory attention, often hearing sounds others may miss.

- Is sensitive to environmental noises and natural sounds.

- Responds emotionally to rhythms and tones.

- Has the ability to recognize, remember, and reproduce musical arrangements and tonal patterns.

- Can create tones, rhythms, form, and movement.

- Thinks in sounds and patterns of sounds.

Examples of musical intelligence in the child:

- Often sings, drums, or whistles to herself while doing something else.

- Has strong preference for certain songs or types of music.

- Is sensitive to sounds; may cry when she hears dissonant or intense sounds.

- Finds music soothing.

- Can distinguish subtleties in musical and natural sounds, such as differences between birdcalls or individual instruments in an orchestra.

- Makes up songs or rhythms about anything.

- Sings her spelling words.

- Has an excellent memory for melodies.

- Can tell when a musical note is off-key.

- Often has a pleasant singing voice.

- Knows the words to many songs.

VISUAL-SPATIAL: This is the ability we have to perceive the visual details of things and how things relate spatially.

The visual-spatially intelligent child:

- Thinks in pictures and images.

- Communicates with unusual, detailed, and colorful images.

- Has a good sense of direction.

- Can manipulate images and create visual metaphors.

- Problem solves visually.

- Has an active imagination.

- Has excellent visual memory.

- Has aesthetic perceptiveness.

Examples of the visual-spatial child:

- Describes situations and experiences with visual details.

- Sees clear visual images when her eyes are closed.

- Enjoys drawing, sculpting, creating patterns, and designs.

- May like activities that involve assembling things with Legos, blocks, Erector sets, etc.

- Likes mazes, pattern blocks, and puzzles.

- May see details in a picture or scene that others miss.

- Is a good chess player.

- Retains images and may be easily scared by images in movies and books.

- Is good at finding her way in her environment and can often find her way around an unfamiliar environment; is a good map reader.

- Is sensitive to color.

- Prefers books with lots of illustrations.

- Is good at geometry.

- Remembers what she sees.

BODILY-KINESTHETIC: This is our ability to control body movements and handle objects with skill.

The kinesthetic child:

- Exhibits ability to use her body in different skilled ways, either for expression or a goal-oriented activity.

- Has the ability to control body movements and understand the consequences of that movement.

- Has the capacity to handle objects skillfully.

- Shows ability to judge timing, the force and extent of movement, and make adjustments as perceived necessary.

- Exhibits excellent eye-hand coordination and balance.

- Exhibits a knowledge of her placement in space.

Examples of kinesthetic intelligence:

- Is graceful.

- Is a good athlete, dancer, or builder.

- Has excellent expression with skills using her hands, such as sewing or woodworking.

- Often expresses emotions with her body, including gesturing with her hands.

- Reads body language well.

- Uses her body to remember and learn—integrating information while she moves and acts.

- May be a good actor or mime.

- Does not sit still easily.

- Touches things a lot; appreciates the feel and texture of objects.

- Is well coordinated.

- Likes thrilling physical experiences, such as daredevil amusement rides.

INTERPERSONAL: This is our ability to relate to and understand others.

The child with excellent interpersonal intelligence:

- Is empathic—able to perceive and understand the feelings of others.

- Understands others' intentions, desires, and motives even when there has been an effort to hide them.

- Is sensitive to the feeling tone of words, sometimes being more affected by the tone than the words.

- Is fluent in the language of emotions—verbal and nonverbal expression.

- Communicates well with others.

- Can take the perspective of others.

Examples of interpersonal intelligence:

- Is a leader with peers.

- Can respond to the tone of your voice or the look on your face.

- Cries when she experiences the distress of animals.

- Is called on by peers for advice and council.

- Can often describe how a person might feel in a certain situation.

- Is an organizer of others.

- May be the peacekeeper with friends and family, mediating because she can see both sides.

- Is adept at verbal and nonverbal communication.

- Likes to "teach" others.

- Likes social interactions.

- Has numerous close friends.

- Seeks others' help when solving a problem.

- Can analyze the behaviors and motivations of fictional characters and predict plot outcomes.

INTRAPERSONAL: This is the knowledge we have of ourselves.

The child with excellent intrapersonal skills:

- Knows herself well, and possesses an understanding of her role in relation to others.

- Has an awareness of her feelings.

- Exhibits a wisdom about the unconscious.

- Shows an ability to monitor emotions and keep from being overwhelmed.

- Tends to have good reasoning and higher-order thinking skills.

Examples of intrapersonal intelligence:

- May prefer to work alone rather than in groups.

- Has an inner clarity or comfort that allows her to be true to her own feelings.

- Needs less approval from peers.

- Has an ability to bounce back from upset or disappointment and learn from the experience.

- Expresses feelings appropriately.

- Recognizes her own strengths and weaknesses.

- Is interested in understanding herself and reflecting on life's questions.

- Is reflective in general.

- Is content to be alone with herself and may appear shy.

- Shows an interest in the spiritual or metaphysical world.

- Has emotional maturity.

NATURALISTIC: This is the sensitivity, understanding, and appreciation we have for the natural world.

The child with strong naturalistic intelligence:

- Loves to be outdoors hiking, camping, gardening, or star gazing.

- Has an affinity for animals.

- Likes to collect things in nature such as leaves, birds' nests, flowers, or rocks.

- Is fascinated by stories in *National Geographic* and the Discovery Channel, or biographies of Jane Goodall or Lewis and Clark.

- Closely looks at things she finds in nature.

Examples of naturalistic intelligence:

- Understands the connection between all living things.

- Can recognize and classify different species of plants or animals.

- May have expert knowledge or interest in geology, biology, astronomy, oceanography, agriculture, weather, and weather phenomena such as tornados.

- Understands environmental and conservation issues.

- Teaches and influences others about environmental and conservation issues—starts a recycling program at school; plans a garden that attracts birds and butterflies; lobbies for healthier food for the lunch program; organizes a protest of the circus.

- Knows a lot about animals in the wild, and is conscious of her impact on their environment.

- Thinks and evaluates from a global perspective.

EXISTENTIAL: This is our ability to think about our own existence in the context of a bigger picture.

The child with strong existential intelligence:

- Wonders about life's bigger questions such as, "Where do you go when you die?" or "Is there life on other planets?"

- When older, ponders, even tries to answers these questions.

- Frequently asks probing questions and likes philosophical discussions.

- Tends to be more serious about his life—concerned with purpose and meaning.

- Thinks about himself and how he fits into the "bigger picture."

- May see or know things he can't explain.

- May have strong interest in mythology, society, and other cultures.

- May have a strong connection to religion and mysticism.

Examples of existential intelligence:

- Connects learning across curricula to the outside world and to his experiences.

- Contemplates phenomena or questions beyond sensory data.

- Has good reflection and abstract reasoning abilities.

- Is intuitive.

- Considers the context of information before determining meaning or implications.

- Relates to the energy or "life force" of activities such as martial arts.

- Influences others to consider meaning and purpose of their lives (such as a theologian).

- Possesses "psychic" abilities or "sixth sense."

- Looks for understanding in the metaphysical world.

Intelligence Truths in a Nutshell

- There is not a direct correlation between IQ and success.

- Some theorists find a correlation between EQ (emotional intelligence) and success.

- There has never been a link made between IQ and fulfillment.

- Most individuals show above-average intelligence in at least one area.

- We may have a particular propensity in two or three areas of intelligence.

- Sometimes one competency is so developed it overshadows all others.

- Memory is not about intelligence.

- Spelling is not about intelligence.

- Faster is not smarter (we can't emphasize this too many times). School is one of the few settings that uses timed tests.

- Intelligence is not static; it can increase or decrease.

- Not being smart is one of our greatest fears.

Appendix
3

Looking at Learning Styles

While expanding our understanding of what intelligence might be, it seems useful to also expand our thinking about how we learn. It follows that different intelligences create different preferences for the way we take in information, or learn. While there can be many factors that influence learning, the current popular model emphasizes learning styles that relate to our senses—specifically, visual, auditory, and kinesthetic. We may receive information through all three senses, but one or two learning styles are usually dominant. Sometimes the dominance changes with the type of task.

What follows are more detailed descriptions of the three predominant learning styles and some specific ways parents can support their children's learning.

AUDITORY OR VERBAL LEARNERS:

- Remember best what they hear.

- Understand best what they hear.

- May be easily distracted by noise or complete silence.

- Prefer verbal instructions.

- Are good listeners.

- Pick up on nuances of language, including tone of voice, pitch, etc. for meaning.

- May move their lips and read out loud.

Ways to assist auditory learners:

- Have a verbal discussion before new experiences, basically telling them what they are going to learn.

- Question children to find out what they know, and then fill in the blanks.

- Debrief activities after they have occurred, helping them make connections and reminding them what they have learned.

- Read things out loud and listen to a tape recorder.

- Do lots of reading, storytelling, or poetry.

- Engage in dramatic play, oral recitation, or music for learning.

- Have them study with a friend or use peer tutoring.

VISUAL LEARNERS:

- Understand best what they see.

- Remember best what they see or read.

- Are distracted by visual obstructions where they cannot see the speaker.

- Pick up on nuances of body language and facial expressions.

- Prefer written instructions.

- Learn well from visual aids, such as diagrams, pictures, and hand-outs.

Ways to assist visual learners:

- Add visual material whenever possible, especially books with pictures for children of all ages.

- Help them create images in their heads of things they have experienced.

- Provide lots of opportunities to create art around their activities.

KINESTHETIC LEARNERS:

- Understand best what they do—what they experience with their hands and body.

- Remember best when it is a hands-on experience.

- Have good motor memory—can remember how to do things after doing them once.

- Have good motor coordination.

- Enjoy lessons that involve active participation or using tools to participate in a practical way.

- Express emotions physically.

- Enjoy acting.

- May have difficulty being still.

Ways to assist kinesthetic learners:

- Allow them to move around while thinking or studying.

- When reading, begin with pictures, headings, or first and last paragraphs, allowing time for them to get a sense of the whole before moving to the details.

- Provide an object such as a Koosh ball to manipulate while sitting.

- Move around while reciting information that you want them to remember.

- Play-act stories in the content areas or literature.

- Try using music to help with studying; research says baroque is especially good.

- Encourage frequent breaks.

- Have them write things they want to learn or remember, possibly just in the air.

- Provide a study place other than a desk, which might be too restrictive.

Appendix
4

Recommended Reading
and Resources

Books Related to Part I

Self-Discovery, Mindfulness, and Voice

The Centering Book: Awareness Activities for Children and Adults to Relax the Body and Mind, by Gay Hendricks and Russel Wills. (Prentice Hall, 1975) This book teaches a variety of centering techniques so that adults and children can experience the solid integration of mind and body and strengthen the connection to their affective, intuitive, and creative processes.

Child's Mind, Mindfulness Practices to Help Our Children Be More Focused, Calm and Relaxed, by Christopher Willard. (Paralax Press, 2010) Not just for children, Willard offers a variety of mindfulness and meditation techniques for individuals and groups that promote awareness, inner balance, and confidence.

Everyday Blessings: The Inner Work of Mindful Parenting, by Jon Kabat-Zinn and Myla Kabat-Zinn. (Hyperion, 1997) This is a beautiful presentation and a thoughtful approach to mindful meditation that will help you slow down, enrich your life as a parent, and nourish the internal life of your children.

Power of Focusing: Finding Your Inner Voice, by Ann Weiser Cornell PhD. (New Harbinger, 1996) This technique of focusing relates to listening to Your Voice, as focusing helps you form a trusting relationship with your body so you can begin to hear its inner wisdom—accessible through body awareness.

Silence: How to Find Inner Peace in a Busy World, by Christina Feldman. (Rodmell Press, 2003) Through photography and poetic text, the subject of silence is explored and celebrated as the pathway to self-discovery and inner calm.

Temperament

Temperament: Theory and Practice (Basic Principles Into Practice), by Stella Chess and Alexander Thomas. (Bruner/Mazel Inc., 1996) This volume takes the reader from the definition of temperament and the studies that support and expand upon that definition, to specific explorations of temperament and its impact across various practice settings and special populations.

Books Related to Part II

Seeing Your Child's Me

The Attachment Parenting Book: A Commonsense Guide to Understanding and Nurturing Your Baby, by Martha Sears and William Sears. (Little Brown & Co., 2001) The Sears discuss how to develop close emotional attachments with your baby and then parent him or her using the insights you gain by virtue of the close bond you share.

Connection Parenting: Parenting Through Connection Instead of Coercion, Through Love Instead of Fear, 2nd Edition, by Pam Leo. (Wyatt-MacKenzie Publishing, 2007) A book discussing nurturing and supporting children through understanding them deeply, respecting their needs, and responding to their communications—i.e., seeing their *Me.*

How to Talk so Kids Will Listen and Listen so Kids Will Talk, Adele Faber and Elaine Mazlish. (Scribner, 1980) This is the first of a few books these authors have written about communication and relationship building between parents and children, and between siblings.

Parenting from the Inside Out, by Mary Hartzell and Daniel J. Siegel (Tarcher/Penguin 2003) The authors explore the extent to which our childhood experiences actually shape the way we parent. Drawing from neurobiology and attachment research, they offer parents a step-by-step approach to forming a deeper understanding of their own life stories, which will help them raise compassionate and resilient children.

Parenting Without Power Struggles: Raising Joyful, Resilient Kids While Staying Cool, Calm, and Collected, by Susan Stiffelman. (ATRIA, 2010) This is a perfect companion book to *Parenting in Your Own Voice*. While many similar topics and ideas are discussed, the emphasis is placed on relationship building with your child. The strategy of coming *alongside* him vs. *at* him when seeking cooperation or compliance is particularly helpful.

Secrets of the Baby Whisperer: How to Calm, Connect, and Communicate with Your Baby, by Tracy Hogg and Melinda Blau. (Random House, 2001) While Tracy Hogg gives lots of helpful advice about everything from sleeping through the night to creating a routine, our favorite parts focus on developing keen observation and listening skills to help see your baby's "me." A follow-up book looks at the toddler.

Temperament

"The Origin of Personality," by Alexander Thomas, Stella Chess, and Herbert G. Birch. (http://www.acamedia.info/sciences/sciliterature/origin_of_personality.htm) This excellent article outlines the authors' theory of Temperament, defining each temperament trait with examples of how these are expressed in children's daily needs and behaviors.

Raising Your Spirited Child: A Guide for Parents Whose Child Is More Intense, Sensitive, Perceptive, Persistent, and Energetic, by Mary Sheedy Kurcinka. (HarperCollins, 1991) For families with children who have intense temperament profiles, this book is a priceless gift for understanding and managing their mystifying and challenging behavior.

Understanding Your Child's Temperament, by William B. Carey. (Simon & Schuster, 1997) This book explains temperament, the idea of "fit" between your child's temperament and the expectations of others, and the many ways this nonjudgmental, insightful understanding of your child can enlighten your parenting.

Development

Getting to Calm: Cool-headed strategies for parenting tweens and teens, by Laura S. Kastner PhD and Jennifer Wyatt PhD. (Parentnap, 2009) A good and cutting-edge resource for understanding the middle and teen years, getting clear about your role, and feeling more capable and loving as their parent.

The Magic Years: Understanding and Handling the Problems of Early Childhood, by Selma H. Fraiberg. (Scribner, reprint, 1996) This timeless classic from the 1950s brings us vividly into the young child's (birth through age six) world and helps us see from her emotional and cognitive perspective.

New First Three Years of Life: Completely Revised and Updated, by Burton L. White. (Fireside, 1995) This detailed guide to the month-by-month mental, physical, social, and emotional development of infants and toddlers contains information and advice available on raising and nurturing the very young child.

Nurture Shock: New Thinking About Children, by Po Bronson and Ashley Merryman. (Twelve, 2011) A surprising and captivating look at what new research and analysis has taught us about a wide range of child development and socialization topics.

Touchpoints—Birth to Three, by T. Berry Brazelton MD. (Da Capo Press, 2006) Dr. Brazelton's great empathy for the universal concerns of parenthood, and honesty about the complex feelings it engenders, as well as his uncanny insight into the predictable leaps and regressions of early childhood, tell us about development with informative and engaging clarity.

Touchpoints 3 to 6, by T. Berry Brazelton MD and Joshua D. Sparrow MD. (Perseus, 2001) Through delightful profiles of four children with very different temperaments, the authors apply the touchpoints theory to each of the great cognitive, behavioral, and emotional leaps that occur from age three to six, and offer precious guidance to parents facing contemporary pressures and stresses.

The Whole-Brain Child: 12 Revolutionary Strategies to Nurture Your Child's Developing Mind, Survive Everyday Parenting Struggles, and Help Your Family Thrive, by Daniel J. Siegel, MD and Tina Payne Bryson, PhD. (Delacorte Press 2011) While teaching about the child's developing brain in accessible language using stories all parents can relate to, these authors provide practical, doable strategies and guidelines for handling everyday parenting occurrences in ways that support your child's brain development.

Why Do They Act That Way?: A Survival Guide to the Adolescent Brain for You and Your Teen, by David Walsh PhD. (Free Press, 2005) Based largely on new brain research and written with an engaging style, this is often a first choice for parents wanting a window into the adolescent brain and advice on communicating and connecting with their teenagers.

Yes, Your Teen Is Crazy, Loving Your Kid Without Losing Your Mind, by Michael Bradley EdD. (Harbor Press, 2003) Bradley opens our eyes and gives us insight into the teen's world, but also guides us toward self-examination and thinking about how the family dynamic can impact teen behavior.

Your One-Year-Old, Your Two-Year-Old, etc. child development series for ages one through nine, by Louise Bates Ames PhD and Francis Ilg MD. (Dell Publishing 1980s) In this series of individual books from the renowned Gesell Institute, the authors discuss all-important questions that concern the child of each age and examine that stage of development in terms of what new things the child can do, how the child acts with parents and other people, what the child thinks and feels, and much more.

Your Ten- to Fourteen-Year-Old, by Louise Bates Ames PhD, Francis Ilg MD, and Sidney Baker MD. (Dell Publishing, 1989) Another invaluable resource from the Gesell Institute, this time for parents of tweens and young teens.

Intelligence, Learning, and Creativity

The Big What Now Book of Learning Styles: A Fresh and Demystifying Approach, by Carol Barnier. (Emerald Books, 2009) This resource book is chockfull of ideas to tackle all kinds of learning for all kinds of learners.

The Creative Family: How to Encourage Imagination and Nurture Family Connections, by Amanda Blake Soule. (Trumpeter Books, 2008) Amanda Soule presents a wide range of projects and ideas to awaken your family's creativity.

Emotional Intelligence, by Daniel Goleman. (Bantam,1995) While previous psychologists discussed the idea and importance of emotional intelligence (i.e., Salovey and Mayer, 1990) it is Goleman's book that popularized the concept. He makes the case that the intrapersonal and interpersonal skills that constitute emotional intelligence are better indicators of future success than IQ scores.

Frames of Mind: The Theory of Multiple Intelligences, by Howard Gardner (Basic Books, 1983) This groundbreaking book expands our view of intelligence, describing nine different types of intelligences and offering the premise that each of us has a unique profile of intelligence.

In Their Own Way: Discovering and Encouraging Your Child's Multiple Intelligences, by Thomas Armstrong PhD. (Tarcher, revised edition 2000) A helpful guide for identifying your child's unique learning style and strengths, and then using your knowledge to support his best learning.

Last Child in the Woods: Saving Our Children from Nature-Deficit Disorder, by Richard Louv. (Algonquin Books, revised and updated edition, 2008) Punctuating Gardner's later decision to add "nature smart" as the one of the nine intelligences, Richard Louv reminds parents that children thrive, learn, and foster imagination when they spend time in the natural world, engaged in natural play.

A Mind at a Time: America's Top Learning Expert Shows How Every Child Can Succeed, by Mel Levine MD. (Simon & Schuster, 2002) Dr. Levine shows parents and those who care for children how to identify individual learning patterns, explaining how they can strengthen a child's abilities and either bypass or help overcome the child's weaknesses, producing positive results instead of repeated frustration and failure.

Tools of the Mind: The Vygotskian Approach to Early Childhood Education, by Elena Bodrova and Deborah J. Leong. (Prentice Hall, second edition, 2006) A bit academic, but good for those who read *Nurture Shock* and want to learn more about the Tools of the Mind program and the relevance of Vygotsky's work for the development of a child's imagination and executive function (e.g., planning, self-monitoring, organizing, etc.).

Your Child's Strengths: A Guide for Parents and Teachers, by Jennifer Fox M.Ed. (Penguin, 2008) A guide and workbook for discovering, appreciating, and encouraging all your child's gifts, big and small—and maybe identifying some of your own in the process.

Books Related to Part III

Fires in the Mind, by Kathleen Cushman. (Wiley, 2012) In this small volume, kids get to tell adults what motivates them to learn and become experts. As parents create parenting plans for their children, it may be helpful to hear the wisdom of these voices.

Mind in the Making: The Seven Essential Life Skills Every Child Needs, by Ellen Galinsky. (HarperCollins, 2010) As you embark on Part III and consider your parenting role, this is a great resource for thinking about what's important to learn and emphasize in the early years.

The Power of Play: Learning What Comes Naturally, by David Elkind, PhD. (Da Capo Press, 2007) With up-to-date research, Dr. Elkind explains the importance of play and the types of play activities that prepare children for learning and provide the most beneficial developmental effects.

The Radical Acceptance of Everything, by Ann Weiser Cornell, PhD. (Calluna Press, 2005) A continuation of Cornell's book about the technique of focusing, with emphasis placed on the concept of acceptance being a first step to change or joy.

Unconditional Parenting: Moving from Rewards and Punishments to Love and Reason, by Alfie Kohn. (Atria Books, 2006) This book invites parents to question their most basic assumptions about raising kids, while offering a wealth of practical strategies for shifting from "doing to" to "working with" parenting—including how to replace praise with the unconditional support that children need to grow into healthy, caring, responsible people.

Other Books Referred to in
Parenting in Your Own Voice

Blink: The Power of Thinking Without Thinking, by Malcolm Gladwell
(Back Bay Books, 2007)

The 7 Habits of Highly Effective People, by Stephen R. Covey
(Free Press, 2004)

Other Recommended Resources

Bank Street Bookstore: 610 W. 112th Street, New York, New York 10025
(at Broadway) Phone orders and info: 212-678-1654 or visit the website at
www.bankstreetbooks.com. Two floors with more than 60,000 books for
kids, parents, and educators and a staff as knowledgeable and helpful as the
selections are awesome and diverse.

Chinaberry catalogue for books for parents and children of all ages
(www.chinaberry.com)

HeartSong catalogue for products to inspire creativity and imaginative play
(www.heartsong.com)

How to Find Good Online Parenting Resources

There is an enormous amount of information available on the web addressing any imaginable issue, ailment, etc. Here are some guidelines to help you
to sort through them.

- Find out who created the website. Who is the source of information?
  Is it a company with a potential conflict of interest, or a neutral

medical or scientific board? Does it cite credible sources in its articles and blogs?

- When addressing medical, psychological, or educational issues, try to rely on websites of institutions such as nih.gov or nimh.gov, or those of reputable universities, with web addresses ending in .edu. This tells you that the articles and information are typically research based.

- Consider information that does not have scientific/research references to be personal opinion or bias. You may decide that you want advice from a known/reputable specialist because you respect his or her opinion. For that, explore their individual websites.

- Be wary of unknown individuals presenting their opinions or trying to sell services or products.

Here are a few websites parents have found helpful:

- hudsonvalleyparents.com/forum/index.php

- childdevelopmentinfo.com

- parentingtoday.org

- www.parentsconnect.com

- www.nick.com

About the Authors

Joan Reynolds MS is a parenting coach and reading specialist with an MS from Bank Street College. For more than two decades, she has worked with children and families in her specialty, and has been a guidance counselor, school learning consultant, and child advocate. In addition, Joan has helped build libraries in low-income communities, taught nutrition and cooking with mothers and children, and conducted weekly story hours for children and parents. Most important, Joan is the mother of a 31-year-old daughter, a role she "continues to grow in." She has had a lifelong interest in helping children reach their potential and believes the best way to help a child is by helping their parents.

Sheila Dinaburg-Azoff PsyD is a parenting coach and holds a doctorate in pediatric/school psychology from Yeshiva University, Ferkauf School of Psychology. For more than two decades, she has worked in hospitals, schools, and clinics running parenting groups, counseling parents and children, and conducting evaluations of children. She has made numerous presentations to parents and professionals on such topics as Therapy with Children, Children and Mourning, Child Development, Self-Esteem, and Parenting Preschoolers. In her view, parents are the experts regarding their children. She has found that through focused discussion, parents can draw upon their insights to expand their understanding of their child. As the mother of two daughters, ages 20 and 24, she continues the learning adventure of being a parent.

Together, Sheila and Joan lead parenting groups and offer workshops based on the process they developed in *Parenting in Your Own Voice*. Their workbook is designed to give parents a structure to do this work on their own or to create their own supportive parenting groups, if they wish. Sheila and Joan are available to meet with your parenting group to help facilitate it in the beginning or along the way. Contact them at info@parentinginyourownvoice.com.